CART'S TOP 200 Adult Books for Young Adults

CART'S
TOP 200

ADULT BOOKS FOR
YOUNG ADULTS

TWO DECADES IN REVIEW

MICHAEL CART

An imprint of the American Library Association // Chicago // 2013

MICHAEL CART is a nationally known expert in young adult literature, which he taught at UCLA before moving to the Midwest. A columnist and reviewer for ALA's *Booklist* magazine, he is also the author or editor of twenty books and countless articles that have appeared in the *New York Times*, the *Los Angeles Times*, the *San Francisco Chronicle*, *Parents* magazine, *American Libraries*, *School Library Journal*, and elsewhere. The former president of both YALSA and ALAN, Cart is the recipient of the 2000 Grolier Award and the first recipient, in 2008, of the YALSA/ Greenwood Publishing Group Service to Young Adults Award. He appointed and chaired the task force that created the Michael L. Printz Award, and he subsequently chaired the 2006 Printz Committee.

© 2013 by the American Library Association. Any claim of copyright is subject to applicable limitations and exceptions, such as rights of fair use and library copying pursuant to Sections 107 and 108 of the U.S. Copyright Act. No copyright is claimed for content in the public domain, such as works of the U.S. government.

Printed in the United States of America

17 16 15 14 13   5 4 3 2 1

Extensive effort has gone into ensuring the reliability of the information in this book; however, the publisher makes no warranty, express or implied, with respect to the material contained herein.

ISBNs: 978-0-8389-1158-7 (paper); 978-0-8389-9625-6 (PDF); 978-0-8389-9626-3 (ePub); 978-0-8389-9627-0 (Kindle). For more information on digital formats, visit the ALA Store at alastore.ala.org and select eEditions.

Library of Congress Cataloging-in-Publication Data
Cart, Michael.
  Cart's top 200 adult books for young adults : two decades in review / Michael Cart.
      pages cm
  Includes bibliographical references and index.
  ISBN 978-0-8389-1158-7
  1. Teenagers—Books and reading—United States—Bibliography. 2. Best Books—United States. I. Title. II. Title: Cart's top two hundred adult books for young adults. III. Title: Top 200 adult books for young adults.
  Z1037.C335 2013
  011.62—dc23
                        2012027260

Cover design by Casey Bayer. Cover image © Timofeyev Alexander / Shutterstock, Inc. Text design by Adrianna Sutton in Minion Pro and Gotham.

♾ This paper meets the requirements of ANSI/NISO Z39.48-1992 (Permanence of Paper).

For Amanda and Alex

CONTENTS

INTRODUCTION

I took my first professional job in 1967, working as the assistant director of the Logansport–Cass County (Indiana) Public Library. Yes, that was my hometown library, and as a compulsive browser even as a child, I was thoroughly familiar with its collections, with what they contained and with what they didn't contain. This may be why one of the first tasks I set myself was developing a separate collection of books for teenage readers, a population whose reading needs and interests had previously been met by a few shelves of genre fiction that consisted mainly of romances by the likes of Janet Lambert, Betty Cavanna, and Rosamond du Jardin. Oh, there were also some sports stories, mostly by John R. Tunis; science fiction, mostly by Robert A. Heinlein and Andre Norton; and adventure, mostly by Howard Pease and Jim Kjelgaard. Today we might regard these books as demi-classics in their respective genres—at least contemporary collectors do, judging by the prices they're willing to pay for first editions of them. But back then they seemed to me to be quick, disposable reads, more suitable for elementary school kids than for adolescents.

My opinion may, of course, have been rooted in my own reading development. I had read this type of genre fiction when I was in grade school but when I finished sixth grade, I graduated to the world of adult books. I claim no particular precocity in doing this, since kids had been reading adult books since at least the seventeenth and eighteenth centuries and the publication of books like John Bunyan's *Pilgrim's Progress*, Jonathan Swift's *Gulliver's Travels*, and Daniel Defoe's *Robinson Crusoe*.

I didn't regret saying goodbye to these early teen books, though I never dismissed them as being baby books, as some teenagers have over the years. On the other hand I certainly didn't regard them as having much literary merit or posing any particular challenge to high school–age readers. So where to turn to find the constituents of my new collection? The answer was simple: I turned to adult books.

I was hardly alone in thinking adult books perfectly suitable for teens. The same year (1967) that I was busy forming my collection, G. Robert Carlsen's *Books and the Teen-Age Reader: A Guide for Teachers, Librarians, and Parents* was published. A veteran professor at the University of Iowa where his mentor Doris V. Smith had also taught, Carlsen, an expert on youth and reading, wrote in his landmark work, "In a good public library young adults [ages 12–18] should be encouraged to use all materials."[1] In fact, he believed that by the age of 16 the reader "will have moved into the type of book generally read by adults,"[2] and he devoted nearly two-thirds of his book to adult literature.

Ironically, 1967 was the same year that a new kind of literature began to emerge that was suitable for teenagers; I just didn't know about it then. I'm referring, of course, to young adult literature, which seemed to appear overnight with the publication of two landmark books: S. E. Hinton's *The Outsiders* and Robert Lipsyte's *The Contender*. This literature differed from the earlier teen literature in its unsparing realism and appeal to teens of high school age.

Not knowing this, however, I made adult books the main focus of the new collection, though I did include a selection of the genre fiction mentioned above, knowing that some readers would find it entertaining and accessible.

Joining Carlsen and me in our focus on adult books was ALA, which had been including adult titles on its lists of best books for teenage readers since 1930, when it established its Young People's Reading Round Table (*young people* in this context meant *teenagers*). Because there was no literature for this specific age group at that time, the Round Table's annual list of best books included a sometimes uneasy mix of adult and children's books, ranging from Will James's *Lone Cowboy* to Edna Ferber's *Cimarron*.

This situation continued until 1948 when, acknowledging that 12- to 18-year-olds had no interest in books for children, the list's name was changed to "Adult Books for Young People." In 1966 it was changed again to "Best Books for Young Adults" (BBYA), though the list continued to be exclusively one of adult books until 1973, when the ALA's Young Adult Services Division (now YALSA) began including books published specifically for young adults.

Since that time there has been considerable discussion (some of it heated) over the proper proportion of adult and young adult titles on the list. When I served on BBYA in 1988–89 I nominated as many adult titles as YA titles. Not everyone agreed with that then or would agree with that today. Indeed, some have suggested that adult books should be eliminated altogether.

While this debate has yet to be resolved, YALSA, in 1998, set up a five-year task force relevant to the discussion. Named in honor of pioneering YA librarian Margaret Alexander Edwards, the group's charge was "to plan, organize, and implement a series of lectures and booklists dealing with adult books for young adults."[3] Its members obviously found that adult books played a viable role in the reading lives of YAs, as the project culminated in the adoption of the Alex Award in 2002, an annual list of ten adult books deemed best of the year for young adult readers.

Less clear, however, are the factors the committee is to take into consideration when selecting its award-winning titles. According to the committee's policies and procedures, there are two criteria:

1. Titles are selected for their demonstrated or probable appeal to the personal reading tastes of young adults.
2. Appeal and popularity are not synonymous. In addition to the question of appeal, committee members should consider the following when assessing titles: language, plot, style, setting, dialog, characterization, and design.[4]

These criteria are certainly helpful in evaluating a book once it has come under consideration, but they don't speak to the preliminary issue: what kind of adult books interest and benefit young adults? While there is no absolute answer to the question, some general guidelines apply. In the case of realistic fiction, for example, a young adult should typically be the protagonist, or at least the major secondary character. This is true whether the book is plot-driven, like Ian Caldwell and Dustin Thomason's *The Rule of Four*, in which two college students struggle to solve the mysteries of an ancient manuscript, or character-driven, like David Mitchell's *Black Swan Green*, about a British boy who is a secret poet.

Second, the book must address situations and concerns that are relevant to young adults' lives or interests. James Finney Boylan's *Getting In*, a comic novel about the Byzantine process of getting into the college of your choice, is a good example. Plot-driven fiction (novels with strong story lines) remains important to YA readers, too. Some of the best examples can be found in genre fiction:

- Helen Fielding's wildly funny British romance *Bridget Jones's Diary,* which inspired the genre now known as chick lit
- Katherine Neville's *The Eight,* a mystery about a young woman's perilous search for a fabled chess set that, legend has it, once belonged to the Emperor Charlemagne
- Neil Gaiman's fantasy *Stardust,* the charming tale of a boy who enters the realm of Faerie in search of a falling star

- Connie Willis's wacky *To Say Nothing of the Dog,* featuring a terribly time-lagged young man who travels back to the year 1888 in search of a monstrosity called the Bishop's Bird Stump
- Matt Haig's *The Radleys,* a horror tale about "ordinary" next door neighbors who just happen to be vampires
- Larry Doyle's *I Love You, Beth Cooper*, in which a nerdy high school senior publicly declares his love for the school's chief cheerleader

Teens also like nonfiction, which is sometimes even more popular than fiction. According to Richard Abrahamson and Betty Carter, the most popular form of nonfiction among teens is the biography, followed by the interview.[5] Not surprisingly, then, Rick Bragg's *All Over but the Shoutin'*, about the Pulitzer Prize–winning journalist's poverty-stricken childhood in the American South, and Andie Dominick's *Needles*, which describes Dominick's lifelong struggle with diabetes, both won Alex Awards.

Other types of nonfiction popular with young adult readers include these:

Accounts of great adventures, such as Jon Krakauer's *Into Thin Air* and Sebastian Junger's *The Perfect Storm*, two best sellers about, respectively, a doomed ascent of Mount Everest and a violent storm at sea. The appeal of these books is their fast narrative pace, lively characterization, suspense (will the subjects live or die?), and overall readability.

Narrative nonfiction, which employs fiction techniques to tell a story while respecting the integrity of factual information. Good examples are Larry Colton's *Counting Coup*, which follows the fortunes of a girls' basketball team on the Crow Indian Reservation in Montana; and Erik Larson's *The Devil in the White City*, the tumultuous story of the 1893 Chicago World's Fair.

Books about subjects of current interest to teens, such as Jaron Lanier's *You Are Not a Gadget*, a cautionary look at the pervasiveness of contemporary computer culture; and Bill McKibben's *Eaarth*, about the dangers of global warming. Other subjects might include computer gaming, sports, and books about teens themselves, like Dave Cullen's *Columbine*.

Nonfiction horror, a spillover from one of the hottest fiction genres. Books about "real-life vampires" are numerous: Joe Garden's *The New Vampire's Handbook*, a tongue-in-cheek guide for "the recently turned creature of the night"; Stephanie Boluk and Wylie Lenz's *Generation Zombie*, a collection of essays about "the living dead"; Linda S. Godfrey's *Werewolves: Mysteries,*

Legends, and Unexplained Phenomena (everything you wanted to know about the man-beast and more!).

Graphic novels. Since the late 1990s the graphic novel format has become wildly popular among young adults, and most public libraries now stock such books. Technically all graphic novels are nonfiction (and cataloged as a form of art by many libraries), but there are plenty of informational graphic novels: *Epileptic*, by David B., a memoir of growing up with an epileptic brother; and Lynda Barry's autobiographical *One Hundred Demons*. Thanks to imprints like First Second Books and Scholastic's Graphix, titles are now being published specifically for young adults. However, the lion's share are still published for adults, and because some graphic novels are, well, graphic, book selectors should never rely entirely on reviews when making purchasing decisions. They should visit a local bookstore or, even better, a comics store (every community in America seems to have one of these) and actually examine the book before they purchase it.

Offbeat nonfiction—those attention-grabbing books about unusual subjects. Two good choices are Steve Almond's *Candyfreak*, the story of the author's lifelong obsession with chocolate; and David Bodanis's *The Secret Family*, in which Bodanis literally examines the world of a typical family under a microscope. The "ick" factor of some of these books make them especially popular with male readers: Mary Roach's *Stiff* reveals what happens to some of us after we die—that is, to our corpses. Ick.

A NEW YOUNG ADULT AND A NEW PUBLISHING PARADIGM

Along with changes in books young adults read have come questions about who's reading them. Traditionally the term *young adult* has referred to those ages 12–18, but given the burgeoning "adultescent" phenomenon, it may now be time to extend that age range.

Consider that nearly fifteen million, or 52 percent, of America's 27.8 million 18- to 24-year-olds are still living at home with their parents, delaying marriage until their late 20s, and refusing to consider a career path job (if they can find one in today's economy, that is) until their early 30s.[6] Many doctors are calling this phenomenon the "second decade of adolescence," noting it begins at 18 and extends to age 24—some suggest even age 28. Despite the age disparity with traditional teens, these adultescents continue to be heavily invested in teen popular culture, shop at the same stores as their younger counterparts, dress the same way, go to the same movies and concerts, and be similarly devoted to every aspect of the burgeoning social media. Like Peter Pan, they simply won't grow up.

So widespread has this phenomenon become that I have suggested, in recent articles and books, that there now exist three literatures for readers moving out of children's books: middle-school literature for 10- to 14-year-olds, teen literature for 12- to 18-year-olds, and what I now call *young adult literature* for 19- to 24-year-olds.

Underscoring the importance of this young adult market is the fact that publishers of adult books are increasingly offering books that will also appeal to teen readers. Two classic examples of adult books with significant teen appeal are Yann Martel's *Life of Pi*, a wonderfully imaginative novel about a boy trapped in a lifeboat with a 450-pound Bengal tiger, and Mark Haddon's *The Curious Incident of the Dog in the Night-Time*, in which a boy with Asperger's syndrome recounts his efforts to solve a mystery.

That these books have multigenerational appeal invites the question, who decides if they are to be published as adult or as young adult? The answer, increasingly, is the publisher's sales and marketing department, often in consultation with the Brobdingnagian bookseller Barnes & Noble. Thus the final decision is made on the basis of not the content of the book but, rather, its sales potential. Will it do better with adult or young adult buyers? Why aren't simultaneous editions published as they are in Great Britain? American publishers are reluctant to say, but the reason is, again, economic. Adult and juvenile departments are separate economic entities, each required to produce a certain level of income every year. As a result, neither is willing to share book profits with the other. This situation also exists at Barnes & Noble, explaining, at least in part, why the bookseller refuses to place a book in more than one section of its stores.

Literature for young adults (however you define it) is inherently dynamic, and likely major changes will happen in the near future. In the meantime, you will find a number of crossover books in the lists that follow.

FINDING REVIEWS

Where should you go to find adult books for your young adult readers? You can start with the three major young adult review media: *Booklist*, *School Library Journal*, and *VOYA*. Each of the publications includes reviews of adult books for young adults, but presents them in a different way. *Booklist* includes an added note to adult titles deemed to be of interest to this readership; *School Library Journal* features a separate section of adult books for young adults in its Book Review section. And *VOYA* uses the code "A/YA" to identify any "adult-marketed book recommended for teens."[7]

All three have been providing this service for a number of years. But how much longer will they be able to continue? Despite the importance of reviews of new titles, print forms of traditional review media are suffering from the downturn in the economy and migration of print to the Web. Some journals are responding with online publication; others are in danger of becoming extinct. General-interest magazines are suffering as well—though, like newspapers, many now publish online editions, often with content different from the print versions. Since it's important for book selectors to examine more than one review before purchase, these media are valuable adjuncts to the professional journals. The books reviewed are often popular fiction and nonfiction that offer opportunities for pleasure reading and feature topics of special interest to teens. Whether in print or electronic form, reliable sources of reviews include the *New Yorker, Atlantic Monthly, Harper's, Entertainment Weekly, Time,* and *Newsweek.* The online magazines *Slate* and *Salon* also have good book coverage.

Another new electronic phenomenon that is changing the world of book reviewing is the growing presence of blogs (a contraction of *web log*). As recently as five years before this book was published blogs about children's and young adult books were a rarity; the field has since exploded. A June 2012 search of the website KidLitosphere Central reveals a strapping total of 728 active blogs—up from three hundred in January 2010.[8] Exact statistics for adult book blogs are harder to find, but as of this publication there are 17,258 members of the website Book Blogs.[9]

Many blogs don't feature traditional book reviews. However, their highly personal, idiosyncratic commentary—which is often unedited, sometimes controversial, and sometimes ill informed—is changing the way people define reviews (and reviewers). Major newspapers include at least one blog as part of their book coverage, as do professional review journals such as *Booklist* and *Library Journal.* These blogs are more reliable sources of information and opinion than the independent versions.

A number of review journals license their reviews to one or both of the two major online bookstores: Amazon.com and Barnes & Noble (www.barnes andnoble.com). Unfortunately, YA notes from *Booklist* are not included on these sites, though they are available to subscribers of Booklist Online (www .booklistonline.com). Because Amazon.com and Barnes & Noble include multiple reviews, it may seem more efficient to consult these sites instead of searching individual magazines for specific reviews. On the other hand, professional review sources include a good many book-related features not available at Amazon.com or Barnes & Noble, such as author interviews, bibliographies, and read-alike suggestions.

Another less-than-salutary phenomenon in the world of book reviewing, introduced by Amazon.com and Barnes & Noble, is the self-posted reader review. Just as anyone with a computer can start a blog, so can he or she post a book review. It almost goes without saying that the quality and reliability of these reviews vary wildly. Like blog reviews, they are largely unedited. In addition, many are posted by people who obviously haven't read the book or are friends of the author. Some have been written pseudonymously by the author.

Given the popularity of social networking, it seems likely these sites will be the next major home for book reviews, whether the sites are generic (Facebook, Twitter) or subject-specific (Goodreads, LibraryThing). Here again, the problem is reliability. Consider a Google search for the phrase *children's and young adult book reviews*. You will get an overwhelming 14,200,000 hits. Learning how to select from this surfeit of . . . stuff, and to evaluate those findings, is clearly becoming a fundamental part of every nascent librarian's education, and poses a challenge for those combing the Web for adult books suitable for young adult readers.

If you go the online route, I'd suggest beginning with the *Booklist* and *School Library Journal* websites. Both contain reliable, staff-written blogs. *Booklist's Book Group Buzz*, for example, includes tips, reading lists, and literary news. *Booklist* editor Keir Graff's online *Likely Stories* addresses book reviewing and the publishing industry. *School Library Journal* offers Angela Carstensen's column, *Adult Books for Young Adults*.

NOTES

1. G. Robert Carlsen, *Books and the Teen-Age Reader: A Guide for Teachers, Librarians, and Parents* (New York: Bantam Books, 1967), 8.
2. Ibid., 29.
3. Beth Yoke, YALSA executive director, e-mail message to author, June 18, 2012.
4. YALSA, Alex Award Committee Policies and Procedures, Suggested Selection Criteria, American Library Association, last revised March 2010, www.ala.org/yalsa/booklistsawards/bookawards/alexawards/alexawardpolicies/.
5. Richard F. Abrahamson and Betty Carter, "Back to the Future with Adult Books for the Teenage Reader," *Journal of Youth Services in Libraries* 11, no. 4 (Summer 1998).
6. Jane Clifford, "Refilling the Nest," *San Diego Union Tribune*, August 20, 2005, E1.
7. VOYA, "VOYA's Review Codes," www.voya.com/reviewers/our-review-codes/.
8. KidLitosphere Central, "Publisher/Editor/Group Blogs," www.kidlitosphere.org/groups/.
9. Book Blogs, "All Members," http://bookblogs.ning.com/profiles/members.

ABOUT THIS BOOK

I love book lists, especially annotated ones, and I suspect I'm hardly the only one who does. Reading them is like browsing the shelves of a well-stocked library. Whether they're relatively brief, such as Anthony Burgess's *99 Novels: The Best in English Literature since 1939* (a partial inspiration for this book) or massive volumes, such as Jacque Barzun and Wendell Hertig Taylor's *A Catalogue of Crime*, they're catnip to me.

Choosing the books to include in this book was—to fearlessly employ a cliché—like a treasure hunt. I started by revisiting the adult books I had reviewed since 1994 when I began reviewing for *Booklist*. I then combed through the files I had assembled during my two terms on the Alex Award committee; I went on to search back issues of the three major youth review media, *Booklist*, *School Library Journal*, and *VOYA*. I consulted other book lists and readers' guides and surveyed lists of award-winning books; I browsed in bookstores, got lost in the maze that is Amazon.com, and finally came up with a list of twice as many books as I could use. Then came the process of some more reading, reading, and reading followed by winnowing and discarding, until I had assembled the list of two hundred fiction and nonfiction titles you'll find here.

Then came the writing, writing, writing of annotations that contain both descriptive and critical content. Somewhere in this process it occurred to me that it might be useful to include a note as to which genre (or, more likely, genres) the titles might fall into.

Here's the list of categories I came up with:

ADV = adventure and exploration
ALEX = Alex Award winner
B/M = biography and memoir
GF = general fiction
GN = graphic novel
GNF = general nonfiction
HIST = history and historical fiction
HOR = horror

HUM = humor
LOI = literature of inclusion
M/S = mystery/suspense
P = poetry
ROM = romance
SCI = science and nature
SPEC = speculative fiction
SPO = sports
TECH = technology

As you can see, I decided, in the interest of economy, to use "symbols" to include with the annotations rather than spelling out the words, especially since many of the annotations include more than one category. We live in an era so notable for its genre bending and blending that it's difficult to assign a title to only one category and consider the case closed. Trust me, it's not.

There are two categories that I decided not to use, thinking they didn't fit the logic of my list. They were "Something Entirely Different" and "Not to Be Missed." Since I couldn't bear to let go of these two altogether, you'll find my lists of them in the appendixes. "Something Entirely Different" is a salute to originality (which becomes increasingly important to me after some sixty-plus years of reading what has come to seem like the same book over and over) and "Not to Be Missed" is, well, a salute to overall excellence. As you might expect, these categories also bend and blend, so some entries appear on both lists.

What more is to be said? Nothing—except that I hope you'll enjoy reading this book as much as I did writing it, and further, that you'll also find it useful!

FICTION

THE ALIENIST

Carr, Caleb. Random House, 1994. ISBN: 0679417796. **HIST, M/S**

The year is 1896, and the mutilated body of a murdered adolescent male prostitute has been discovered on the Williamsburg Bridge over New York's East River. In an unorthodox move, the newly appointed police commissioner Theodore Roosevelt (yes, the future president) asks two nonpolice personnel—John Schuyler Moore, a *New York Times* reporter, and Dr. Laszlo Kreizler, an alienist (as psychologists were then called)—to investigate. Their methods are equally unorthodox. Discovering that the murderer is a homicidal maniac who has perpetrated similar crimes, the two "detectives" use the details of these to develop a psychological profile that, they hope, will lead them to the killer. This intellectual approach and careful attention by the author to period details will remind some readers of the Sherlock Holmes adventures—in spirit if not in execution.

This novel has been enormously popular with YAs, as has its sequel: *The Angel of Darkness* resembles the first novel but boasts more real historical figures. A woman, an alleged serial killer, is defended at her trial by no less than attorney Clarence Darrow. Fans of E. L. Doctorow (think *Ragtime*) will enjoy both of these unusual novels.

ALL SOULS

Schutt, Christine. Harcourt, 2008. ISBN: 9780151014491. **GF**

Astra Dell, the "star" of her senior class at the exclusive Siddons School on Manhattan's Upper East Side, is ill with a mysterious ailment that might well prove fatal. The novel that grows up around her focuses on the impact her illness has on various classmates, teachers, and parents. An English teacher at a private school in New York, Schutt brings a rare understanding of that milieu to this excellent novel along with the psychological insights that enrich her characters. The author's novel *Florida* was shortlisted for the National Book Award in 2004, and her literary skills are once again in evidence in *All Souls*, including her narrative strategy, which is to tell her story from multiple points of view in impressionistic snippets of story that are notable for their brevity (some are no longer than a paragraph). The cumulative power of the story is, however, significantly larger than the sum of its parts. Readers who have enjoyed this novel may wish to have a look at Paul Murray's somewhat similar take on prep school life *Skippy Dies*.

ALL THE PRETTY HORSES /
THE CROSSING / CITIES OF THE PLAIN

McCarthy, Cormac. Knopf, 1992. ISBN: 0394574745 / Knopf, 1994.
ISBN: 0394574753 / Knopf, 1998. ISBN: 0679423907. **HIST**

It's nearly impossible to summarize the three volumes that comprise McCarthy's Border Trilogy series—at least in a brief space. McCarthy is one of America's greatest novelists, as he has proven in such masterpieces as *Blood Meridian* and *The Road*. And some of his work requires considerable literary sophistication of its readers. These three linked novels are more accessible, however, and since they feature teenage protagonists, they are of intrinsic interest to YAs. Volume 1, *All the Pretty Horses*, which won the National Book

Award, is set in the immediate post–World War II years in West Texas. It's the coming-of-age story of 16-year-old rancher John Grady Cole, who, losing his prospective inheritance, sets off to Mexico to find a new life and, perhaps, a new fortune. Volume 2, *The Crossing*, is set a decade earlier and tells the story of another 16-year-old, Billy Parham, who is growing up on a ranch in southern New Mexico. Like John, he too will head to Mexico with uneven results. Volume 3, *Cities of the Plain*, is set in the early 1950s and brings John and Billy together, working as ranch hands on the same spread. There is a melancholy air to this novel, which acknowledges the impending death of a Western way of life. Like the first two it will take its protagonists back to Mexico, this time to rescue a young Mexican prostitute from her vicious pimp. There are tragic elements to this great American trilogy and certain aspects are inarguably depressing, but the experience of reading such beautifully written work redeems the novels from that and further establishes McCarthy's place at the very top tier of great American writers. That *All the Pretty Horses* was made into a movie starring Matt Damon and Penelope Cruz will doubtless expand the audience for the first volume of this trilogy.

THE AMAZING ADVENTURES OF KAVALIER AND CLAY

Chabon, Michael. Random House, 2000. ISBN: 0679450041. **GF, SPEC, HIST**

Amazing, indeed—amazing enough to win the Pulitzer Prize in fiction! Chabon, the author of such celebrated works of fiction as *The Mysteries of Pittsburgh* and *Wonder Boys*, has outdone himself in this epic fictional treatment of the early days of comic book publishing in America, beginning in the 1930s and continuing through the early 1950s. Chabon brings an exuberance to this work that is infectious and tinges it with elements of magical realism. Following an ingenious escape from Nazi-controlled Czechoslovakia, Joe Kavalier travels circuitously to Brooklyn, there to join his young cousin Sammy Clay. Together the two young men then create a masked comic book superhero called the Escapist. The name reflects not only the Escapist's mission—to help people everywhere escape oppression—but also Joe's own exodus from Europe, his background in magic, and his penchant for wandering. Chabon did prodigious research to bring to life the mechanics, the business, and the politics of early comic book publishing that will fascinate not only fanboys but also the general reader. In the process he became so fascinated himself with the subject that, in the wake of the novel, he created a comic book series of his own titled *Michael Chabon Presents the Amazing Adventures of the Escapist*. Published by Dark Horse Comics, the series received the prestigious Eisner Award for best comics anthology of 2004. Truly amazing!

ANTHILL

Wilson, Edward O. Norton, 2010. ISBN: 9780393071191. **GF**

Wilson, who is one of the world's leading authorities on ants and the winner of two Pulitzer Prizes for his nonfiction, has here written his first novel, and the result is remarkable. It begins with the story of a boy named Raphael (Raff) Semmes Cody, who falls between two worlds—his mother's one of wealth and privilege and his father's of working-class redneck life. The boy finds refuge in exploring the world of the Nokobee Swampland in Florida's panhandle, where he meets a Florida State professor named Fred Norville, who helps shape Raff's education, which culminates in a law degree from Harvard. Returning to his home state of Alabama, Raff launches an effort to save the endangered Nokobee wilderness. Oddly/interestingly/fascinatingly enough, Wilson has included a seventy-page section in the middle of the novel devoted to the life and death of an ant colony; the conceit being that this is Raff's dissertation, though many readers will suspect it is Wilson's excuse for focusing attention on his own scientific specialty (his book *Ants* was one of his Pulitzer Prize winners). Whatever the reason, it is a fascinating diversion and could be published as a stand-alone monograph. The novel's surprise ending is sure to engender much passionate discussion. Readers who enjoy this novel might want to have a look at some of the mysteries of Carl Hiaasen, who focuses most of them on the continuing war between those who wish to exploit Florida's unspoiled areas and those who wish to preserve them.

AS SIMPLE AS SNOW

Galloway, Gregory. Putnam, 2005. ISBN: 0399152318. **M/S, ALEX**

Snow is simple? Sure it is: about as simple as this tantalizingly complex mystery. Here's the premise: an average high school boy—the narrator—falls in love with Anna, a mysterious goth girl whose hobby is writing obituaries of everyone in their small town. Yes, the people aren't dead yet but, as the girl observes, "it's only a matter of time." The first to die, however, is Anna herself.

Or does she die? Certainly she vanishes, leaving behind only a dress next to a hole in the river ice. Refusing to believe she's dead, however, the narrator determines to find her and soon finds himself up to his eyebrows in a jumble of the kinds of codes, ciphers, mysteries, and ghost stories that spooky Anna loved. Evocative of Rod Serling's classic *Twilight Zone* television series, Galloway's first novel will intrigue some and frustrate others; but with its head-scratching forebodings and foreshadowings, its complexities and conundrums, it's bound to remain in the memory of everyone who reads it.

ATONEMENT

McEwan, Ian. Doubleday/Talese, 2002. ISBN: 0385503954. **HIST**

Like Cormac McCarthy, the British writer Ian McEwan generally takes no prisoners, demanding his readers invest serious attention to the material at hand. In this case it's the character-driven story, opening in 1935 on a British country estate, of two young people. Cecilia is the daughter of an upper-class British family, while Robbie is the son of the family's cleaning lady. When Cecilia's younger sister, Briony, a would-be writer, happens to witness an ambiguous encounter between Cecilia and Robbie, her imagination runs wild, and she misrepresents the encounter with near disastrous results. The novel then follows its characters through World War II and beyond as the now young adult Briony struggles to make atonement to Cecilia and Robbie for her actions. *Atonement* was shortlisted for the Booker Prize and won the 2002 National Book Critics Circle Award in the fiction category. It was also made into a movie.

BATWOMAN: ELEGY

Rucka, Greg. Illustrated by J. H. Williams III. DC Comics, 2010. ISBN: 9781401226923. **GN, LOI, M/S**

As is often the case with graphic novels, the contents of this trade paperback were originally published as individual stories in *Detective Comics*. Batwoman is gay—a departure from many graphic novel interpretations. The volume gives readers some of her backstory, including her discharge from the military because of her sexual identity. It then flashes forward to the present, wherein Batwoman encounters the dubious Alice, who evokes Alice in Wonderland

and, indeed, speaks only in quotations from Lewis Carroll. It makes for an attractively dark and compelling story, but critics are unanimous in suggesting that Williams's stunning art nouveau illustrations are equally important to the success of this volume, and they will get no argument from this quarter. This title was selected for ALA's Rainbow Project bibliography, an annual list of the best youth books with GLBTQ content.

THE BIG BOOK OF ADVENTURE STORIES

Penzler, Otto, ed. Vintage, 2011. ISBN: 9780307474506. **ADV**

A big book of adventure stories that range from Tarzan of the Apes to Hopalong Cassidy and from island paradise settings to deadly deserts. Armchair adventurers will be entranced. What more is there to say?

BLACK HOLE

Burns, Charles. Pantheon, 2005. ISBN: 037542380X. **GN, HOR**

Widely regarded as a modern masterpiece, Burns's deeply disturbing story is the surrealistic account of a sexually transmitted disease called "the bug." It manifests itself as bizarre mutations that disfigure the affected teens, who live in camps in the woods away from society. Burns humanizes his scenario—set in Seattle in the 1970s—by focusing on two teens, Keith and Chris (the latter is a girl) who contract the disease. Both suffer from ghastly nightmares that Burns renders in detail in his vividly realized black-and-white illustrations. He also beautifully captures teen angst and anomie in a near existential setting. Call it atmospheric, call it creepy, *Black Hole* is unforgettable and a book that many teens who read it will regard as a quintessential coming-of-age experience.

BLACK SWAN GREEN

Mitchell, David. Random House, 2006. ISBN: 1400063795. **GF, HIST, ALEX**

When celebrated English author Mitchell was a boy, he suffered from a stammer, an affliction that plagues his protagonist, 13-year-old Jason, in this largely autobiographical novel. Set in the village of Black Swan Green, the novel recounts the boy's desperate attempts to fit in with the other boys and—touchingly—his equally desperate attempts to avoid having to say words that trigger his stammer. Set in 1982, this vaguely episodic novel—each of its thirteen chapters can be viewed as a stand-alone story—features such subjects as the disintegrating nature of his parents' marriage; Jason and his friends' reaction to Britain's invasion of the Falklands and the death of a local soldier; and the community's dealings with Gypsies (which will recall Jeanine Cummins's *The Outside Boy*). One of the most memorable and funniest of these episodes is the story of Jason's encounter with the local Bohemian Mme. Eva van Outryve de Crommelynck, who knows Jason's most closely guarded secret: he is a poet who is being published pseudonymously in a local paper! Jason's innocence makes him an especially appealing character in what promises to become a classic coming-of-age novel. Those who are intrigued by Jason's stammer might want to view the motion picture *The King's Speech*, about King George VI's similar, lifelong problem. British actor Colin Firth won an Academy Award for his portrayal of the king.

BRIDGET JONES'S DIARY

Fielding, Helen. Viking, 1998. ISBN: 0670880728. **ROM, HUM**

If Helen of Troy's was the face that launched a thousand ships, British author Helen Fielding's first novel was the book that launched a new subgenre—chick lit—and a thousand (or more) imitations. It's hard to specify the precise reasons for the novel's resonance (critic Daphne Merkin called it "a cultural artifact that is recognizably larger than itself"), but it surely has something to do with the book's robust humor, with Bridget Jones herself—one of whose goals is to reduce the circumference of each thigh by 1.5 inches—and with the book's form, a journal of a year in the life, including a daily record of calories consumed, cigarettes smoked, lottery tickets bought, alcohol units imbibed, and other seemingly unbreakable bad habits. Readers who are—like Bridget—attempting to lose a number of dubious habits themselves might gain a little perspective from our heroine's many failures: she loses seventy pounds but gains seventy four, indulges in an unwise relationship with her boss, deals with her mother's disappearance with a Portuguese gigolo, and more—much more. Though Bridget is 30-something, teenage readers who cut their teeth on Louise Rennison's teenage Georgia Nicholson will be highly amused by Bridget's peccadilloes and cheered by her unfailing good humor. Look for the sequel, *Bridget Jones: The Edge of Reason.*

THE BRIEF WONDROUS LIFE OF OSCAR WAO

Díaz, Junot. Riverhead, 2007. ISBN: 1594489580. **GF, LOI**

The Dominican American author follows up his acclaimed short story collection *Drown* (1996) with this ambitious novel that achieved the double distinction of winning the National Book Critics Circle Award and the Pulitzer Prize. Michiko Kakutani, chief book critic for the *New York Times*, called it "funny, street smart, and keenly observed." It is all these and more—an often exuberant and sometimes horrifying story of the Dominican diaspora from the dictatorial regime of Rafael Trujillo. Díaz's chief character is the eponymous Oscar, a 307-pound science fiction geek and second-generation immigrant who lives with his family in Paterson, New Jersey. Oscar may claim center stage, but every member of his family steals the spotlight in individual ways. Perhaps because of the richness of its characterization, this beautifully written novel manages—without being in any way tendentious—to show the sad story of the Dominican Republic through the fate of a single family. Without missing a beat, it also takes the reader back in time to the family's homeland. Deeply felt, funny, and poignant, it is an altogether remarkable and unforgettable novel. For another view of the Dominican Republic under Trujillo, see Julia Alvarez's *In the Time of the Butterflies.*

THE CANTERBURY TALES

Chaucer, Geoffrey, and Peter Ackroyd. Viking, 2009. ISBN: 9780670021222. **HIST**

The prolific British author retells the classic Chaucer tales for contemporary readers. This would be a ridiculously overambitious project for most authors, but Ackroyd brings it off with polish and aplomb—not only modernizing the English in terms of spelling and meaning, but also translating Chaucer's verse into prose that is nevertheless poetic instead of prosaic. It helps, of course, that Ackroyd is a biographer of Chaucer and has previously based a novel, *The Clerkenwell Tales*, on Chaucer's immortal saga. It's an altogether lovely tribute to the father of English literature.

CARAMELO
Cisneros, Sandra. Knopf, 2002. ISBN: 0679435549. **GF, LOI**

Best known for her poetry (*Loose Woman*), her short fiction (*Woman Hollering Creek and Other Stories*), and her novel *The House on Mango Street*, Chicana author Cisneros has written an ambitious work of extended fiction (464 pages) that recounts the compelling story of the Reyeses, a multigenerational family that has immigrated from Mexico to Chicago, where the father becomes a furniture upholsterer. This is an affectionate and often funny story of a family caught between two worlds, a family that travels in a caravan of cars each summer to Mexico City to visit the Awful Grandmother and the Little Grandfather. Initially the story is told by the youngest child and only daughter, Lala, and focuses on her childhood and adolescence. The novel soon becomes the story of her ancestors as well, especially the Awful Grandmother, whose acerbic and intrusive comments pepper the narrative. Loosely based on her own childhood, Cisneros's story shines with love of family and fascination with its history. YA readers—and their teachers—who are interested in exploring the work of other successful writers of short fiction who have then produced blockbuster novels night want to have a look at Katherine Anne Porter's *Ship of Fools* and Eudora Welty's *Losing Battles*.

CITRUS COUNTY
Brandon, John. McSweeny's Rectangulars, 2011. ISBN: 9781934781531. **GF**

Citrus County, Florida, lies a couple hours north of St. Petersburg "on what people called the Nature Coast," author Brandon tells us, explaining:

> "There was nature because there were no beaches and no amusement parks and no hotels and no money. There were rednecks and manatees and sinkholes. There were insects, not gentle crickets but creatures with stingers and pincers and scorn in their hearts."

Yes, readers, this is the landscape of Southern gothic fiction, and *Citrus County* is a downright dandy example of this darkly fascinating genre. Not surprisingly, a dark miasma of foreboding hangs over the novel like a shroud over a corpse. The major event of the story is the kidnapping of Shelby's little sister, Kaley. Shelby is the new girl in school; she is quickly and ineluctably drawn to Toby, the resident bad boy who—parentless—lives with his sociopathic uncle.

Aside from their tentative interest in each other, the two teens have in common Mr. Hibma, their 29-year-old geography teacher who dreams of murdering Mrs. Conner, the 50-something "grammar Nazi" English teacher. All righty, then. This is an offbeat and original coming-of-age novel that invites readers to consider whether the events of our lives are momentous or meaningless, whether our endings are really beginnings, and what's the best way to think about the things we've done. Readers who enjoy this will surely want to discover the fiction of the late Flannery O'Connor, the queen of Southern gothic. Her work is available in *Flannery O'Connor: Collected Works*, part of the Library of America series.

THE CLIENT

Grisham, John. Doubleday, 1993. ISBN: 038542471X. **M/S**

Former attorney Grisham's legal thrillers are almost as popular with YAs as Stephen King's stories of horror and their unnerving intersection with reality. There is no "almost" about *The Client*, however. It is clearly one of Grisham's best—and most teen-friendly. When 11-year-old Mark inadvertently witnesses the suicide of a mob-defending attorney, he learns a closely guarded secret about a murdered senator that will put him squarely—and dangerously—between an ambitious, unscrupulous attorney and a mob boss named Barry the Blade. Mark becomes the client of the title when—for a dollar—he retains the legal services of a tyro lawyer named Reggie Love, a divorced, 50ish woman who has been a lawyer for only four years but becomes fiercely protective of—though often impatient with—her new client, who is precocious beyond his years. Though never a darling of the critics, Grisham—as always—shows himself such a master of setting (thanks to his own career as an attorney) and nail-biting suspense that the turning pages become a blur. This was made into a successful 1994 movie starring Susan Sarandon and Tommy Lee Jones.

COFFEE WILL MAKE YOU BLACK

Sinclair, April. Hyperion, 1994. ISBN: 1562827960. **GF, LOI**

Here is another novel that has become a staple for young adult readers making the transition to adult fiction. Set in Chicago in the late 1960s, Sinclair's novel follows the coming-of-age of Jean Stevenson, who is 11 at the book's outset and 15 at its conclusion. While Jean ("Stevie") is experiencing ritual rite of passage experiences—first kiss, first period, and the like—black culture and civil rights are also coming of age, and the story nicely strikes parallels between the societal and the personal (Stevie discovers the work and larger-than-life persons of Martin Luther King and Malcolm X, for example). As racial stereotypes are revealed and rejected, Stevie learns to be proud of her identity and that, in the parlance of the times, "Black is beautiful."

A COMPLICATED KINDNESS

Toews, Miriam. Counterpoint, 2004. ISBN: 1582433216. **GF**

This superb novel tells the coming-of-age story of Nomi Nickel, who lives in a Mennonite community on the plains of Manitoba. Being a Mennonite, she wryly observes, is to live in "the most embarrassing sub-sect of people to belong to if you're a teenager." It's not easy for adults, either. In fact, half of Nomi's family—"the better-looking half," she notes of her absent mother and older sister—have fled life in the repressive community, which shuns modern ways. Nomi's mother had little choice, since she had been excommunicated by her own brother, the local minister, whom Nomi acidly calls "the mouth of darkness." Nomi herself has pot-fueled dreams of escaping the community and moving to New York to become a groupie for Lou Reed (!), but she cannot bring herself to desert her gentle, befuddled father, who is busy selling off all their furniture. Author Toews grew up in a similar community and writes with authority not only of daily life there but also of the large questions that such circumstances invite about the conflict between freedom and religious oppression.

THE CURIOUS INCIDENT OF THE DOG IN THE NIGHT-TIME

Haddon, Mark. Doubleday, 2003. ISBN: 0385509456. **GF, LOI, ALEX**

Here is another modern classic that—along with *Life of Pi*—helped usher in the modern adult crossover novel. First published in England, this is the story of a teenage boy who discovers that his neighbor's dog has been killed by being run though with a pitchfork; he decides he will solve this case as he imagines his hero, Sherlock Holmes, might have done. The boy, 15-year-old Christopher, tells the reader his story in his own first-person voice, which is extraordinary, since Christopher is autistic and author Haddon's imagining of his deadpan tone is a tour de force of narrative choice. Christopher, who lives with

his single-parent father, may be a mathematical genius, but he is totally ignorant of social cues and other people's emotions. This leads to some extremely
funny scenes as the boy overreacts to a policeman's queries and then attempts
to interview neighbors himself in search of clues. As the reader will come to
understand, there is a larger mystery here than the simple case of a murdered
dog. Though Christopher is, at first, completely ignorant of it, his investigation will have the secondary effect of solving this larger puzzle. There has been
considerable discussion in this country about whether this book should have
been published as a YA title. In England it was published in simultaneous YA
and adult editions, which would have been the perfect procedure here. Unfortunately, for economic reasons such simultaneous publication is regarded as
impossible in this country. While this issue remains unresolved, one thing at
least is certain: the appeal of this enchanting book is universal.

DIAMOND DOGS

Watt, Alan. Little, Brown, 2000. ISBN: 0316925810. **GF, ALEX**

Seventeen-year-old Neil Garvin's single-parent father is sheriff of their small
community near Las Vegas. The father's deep-rooted anger and his alcohol
abuse have taken a toll on Neil, who is the star quarterback on his high school
football team and also a relentless bully. Having drunk too much at a party
where he abused two freshmen, he drives home with his lights out and acci-
dentally hits one of the young men, killing him. Not knowing what to do, he
puts the body in the trunk of the car and drives home. In the morning he
discovers, to his horror, that the body is gone. Yes, his father has found the
corpse, and yes, he covers up for his son until the FBI gets involved and things
become increasingly complicated. Watt does a fine job of limning difficult
father-son relationship issues in his first novel, which was selected as an Alex
Award winner. And if you're wondering, the Diamond of the title refers to
pop singer Neil Diamond, the father's favorite performer.

DRINKING COFFEE ELSEWHERE

Packer, Z. Z. Riverhead, 2003. ISBN: 1573222348. **GF, LOI, ALEX**

Packer's marvelous debut collection of eight stories features largely—but not
exclusively—African American protagonists living in Baltimore and Washington, DC, though one especially memorable story is set in Japan. Seven of

the eight protagonists are young women who are confronting—or being confronted by—imposing coming-of-age moments: running away to find one's absent mother, prostituting oneself for food, and encountering racial prejudice. Perhaps the best story in the book deals with that last topic; it's the story of a black Brownie troop who conspire to take revenge on a white troop, one of whose members has used the "n" word—until they confront and actually begin to know the white girls, discovering some surprising truths in the process. This is another Alex Award winner and one that was also a finalist for the PEN/Faulkner Award. Packer is winner of both a Guggenheim Fellowship and a Whiting Writer's Award.

THE EIGHT

Neville, Katherine. Ballantine, 1988. ISBN: 9780345351371. **SPEC**

Here is another of the currently fashionable puzzle-mysteries (see *As Simple as Snow* and *The Rule of Four*). This one involves the Montaigne Service, a mystical chess set that once belonged to the Emperor Charlemagne and that contains a code which—when deciphered—gives its player great powers. The chess pieces, accordingly, were dispersed during the French Revolution. Now—well, in 1972—an accountant and computer expert named Catherine Velis finds herself tasked with recovering the pieces. Needless to say, she's not the only one hot on the trail. Of course, deciphering the code plays a major role in the story that ensues. If readers are wondering, Neville's novel predates *The Da Vinci Code* and may indeed have inspired its theme.

Twenty years after the publication of *The Eight*, a sequel, *The Fire*, appeared. It involves Catherine's daughter, Alexandra, who is searching for her vanished mother. Of course, the chess pieces that drove the plot of *The Eight* appear again. This time a parallel story, set in 1822, involves another young woman whose quest involves Lord Byron. How romantic can you get?

ELECTION

Perrotta, Tom. Putnam, 1998. ISBN: 0399143661. **GF, HUM**

Set in suburban New Jersey in 1992, this darkly humorous story of a high school election was made into a—you guessed it—popular movie starring Matthew Broderick and the incomparable Reese Witherspoon. Here's the story: ambitious high school student Tracy Flick will do anything to be elected president of Winwood High; her chances are diminished, however, when a popular, sweet-spirited jock, Paul Warren, is persuaded to run by Mr. McAllister (Mr. M.), the election faculty adviser who will do anything—well, almost—to forestall Tracy's election. This does not set well with Paul's younger sister, who is in love with Paul's girlfriend, and *she* (the sister) decides to run. Things deteriorate rapidly for poor Mr. M., whose marriage is also in deep trouble. Opportunities to satirize high school life abound and are enhanced by the use of multiple first-person voices. Perrotta is also the author of *Joe College*, which is set in 1980 at Yale University, where outsider Danny, a junior, has to cope with various crises including wealthy students, spring break, a group of extortionists, and, oh, yes, the pregnancy of his girlfriend . . .

ELLEN FOSTER

Gibbons, Kaye. Algonquin, 1987. ISBN: 0912697520. **GF**

An oldie but goodie, this first novel has been a perennial favorite with YAs since its first publication a quarter-century ago. And it's small wonder, since the story is filled with teen-friendly elements, including a spunky heroine who tells her story in her own memorable first-person voice ("When I was little, I would think of ways to kill my daddy") and an involving plot that invites the reader's empathy, particularly when Ellen recalls her terrible childhood with an alcoholic, abusive father (her much loved mother died young) and with relatives who weren't much better. Gibbons is a Southern writer, of course, and telling stories is as easy for her (and her narrator) as normal conversation is for Yankees. Contrary to many stories about kids from unfortunate home situations, it's not until Ellen is placed in a foster home that her life actually improves. Readers who have become emotionally engaged with her will celebrate and pass the book on to a friend. For the record, the book has been a hit not only with readers but with critics as well, receiving universal praise and winning the prestigious Sue Kaufman Prize from the American Academy and Institute of Arts and Letters.

ELMER

Alanguilan, Gerry. SLG, 2010. ISBN: 9781593622046. **GN, SPEC**

Fable and satire meet somewhere in the middle in this offbeat story of sentient chickens that have, for too long, been victimized and exploited by humankind. Part of the story centers on the fowls' determined and sometimes violent struggle for racial equality, but part also examines the domestic life of Jake, whose father, the eponymous Elmer, is dying. This event reunites the family, bringing the son home along with his siblings, a newly engaged sister and a gay movie star brother. Going home again vividly recalls for Jake his difficult childhood and, when he discovers his father's diary after Elmer's death, introduces him to that of his dad as well. The story's beautifully evoked setting is the author/artist's native Philippines, a fact that ensures the landscape will be more than a simple backdrop; it is instead a significant contribution to the tale's ethos.

EXTREMELY LOUD AND INCREDIBLY CLOSE
Foer, Jonathan Safran. Mariner Books, 2005. ISBN: 9780618329700. **GF**

In the wake of the death of Oskar's father in the 9/11 tragedy, the 9-year-old boy discovers a mysterious key belonging to him that is labeled only "black." This sets the determined youngster on a quest throughout New York to find the owner of the key. That this means interviewing every single person with the surname Black doesn't daunt him a bit! Foer's second novel is a brilliant tour de force of imagination that comes in a beautifully designed package—a book that's illustrated with photographs, employs a variety of different typefaces, and ends with a fourteen-page flip book. All of this adds to the attractively offbeat originality that is a hallmark of this novel and is sure to delight young adult readers. A subplot involving Oskar's grandfather, who survived the World War II firebombing of Dresden, Germany, may send readers on a search of their own: to find and read Kurt Vonnegut's classic novel *Breakfast of Champions*, which also features the bombing that, in some ways, prefigures 9/11. (Oh, yes: the character of Oskar is inspired by the protagonist of Gunter Grass's novel *The Tin Drum*, but the reader doesn't necessarily need to know that.) More recently Foer has written *Eating Animals*, a nonfiction book dealing with his ambivalent feelings about meat.

THE FLOWERS
Gilb, Dagoberto. Grove, 2008. ISBN: 9780802118592. **GF, LOI**

This often funny slice-of-life novel tells the story of a 15-year-old Chicano named Sonny Bravo. When his mother marries a bigoted Okie named Cloyd, the family moves into the Flowers (Los Flores), an apartment building that Cloyd owns. Sonny's not unwelcome assignment to perform various menial chores around the building gives him an opportunity to get out of the apartment as well as to meet and interact with various tenants, including Mr. Pinkston, an albino African American, and with other teens like Cindy, a married dropout, and Nica, whose duty to take care of her brother keeps her confined to her own apartment all day. Meanwhile the world outside erupts into the violence of a race riot that viscerally reminds the reader that Sonny lives in a world defined by prejudice and hatreds. Despite its often engaging immediacy, the real draw of this novel is Sonny's first-person voice with its mixture of Spanish and English, its run-on sentences, and its street slang, a combination of elements that makes for hectic but rhythmic music that sticks in the memory.

Gilb is not only a novelist but also a short story writer whose collection *The Magic of Blood* won a PEN/Hemingway Award and an essayist whose *Gritos* was a finalist for the National Book Critics Circle Award.

GETTING IN

Boylan, James Finney. Warner, 1998. ISBN: 9780446674171. **GF, HUM, ALEX**

Getting into the (prestigious) college of your choice has become something of a nightmare these days, what with the stiff competition and the perceived need to assemble a résumé that would rival that of the president of a Fortune 500 corporation. Boylan, however, deftly demonstrates that there is also a humorous side to this process as he puts four high school seniors and three adults into a Winnebago and sends them on a tour of New England campuses—including Colby where he (i.e., the author) teaches and thus brings an insider's knowledge to the admissions chase. As one might expect, Boylan has lots of fun with interviews and suchlike while also demonstrating that his four teens will not only learn about colleges on their tour of academia but also about themselves. You'll find Boylan's surprising memoir *She's Not There* in the nonfiction section. Don't miss it.

GIL'S ALL FRIGHT DINER

Martinez, A. Lee. Tor, 2005. ISBN: 0765311437. **HOR, ALEX**

Rejoice, horror fans. Here's a novel that features not only a vampire but also a werewolf, both of whom are on the trail of a pack of pesky zombies! It doesn't get any better than this. Earl (the vampire) and his bud Duke (the werewolf) set this whole thing into action when they stop, one evening, at Gil's All Night Diner for a bite to eat (not Gil, presumably!). Hardly have they sat down when zombies show up, and the two manage to fight off this onslaught of the undead. Loretta, the proprietor, is good and tired of zombies storming her place and hires Earl and Duke to handle—as it were—pest control. What a teen named Tammy has to do with all this is for me to know and you to find out.

THE GIRL WHO LOVED TOM GORDON
King, Stephen. Scribner, 1999. ISBN: 0684867621. **SPEC, HOR**

King, as mentioned more than once in this book, is arguably the most popular of all the adult authors whose work appeals to teens—quintessentially so. And of all of King's many novels, this one is arguably the most popular with teens (well, a case could probably be made for *Carrie*, as well). Here's the story: the girl in question is 9-year-old Trisha, who one day wanders away from her family while they're hiking the Appalachian Trail (see Bill Bryson for his own nonfiction take on the AT experience). Realizing she is lost, Trisha finds comfort and a connection to civilization by listening on her Walkman to a broadcast of a Boston Red Sox–New York Yankees game in which her favorite Sox player, relief pitcher Tom Gordon, strikes out the eternal rival Yankees. Thereafter Trisha imagines Tom is with her, a comforting presence that keeps her alive as the days pass. But wait! What is that . . . *something* that is secretly following her through the swamp and woods? Welcome, reader, to the world of Stephen King, who, in the book's first sentence, has reminded us, "The world has teeth and it could bite you with them anytime it wanted." Ouch!

GIRL WITH A PEARL EARRING
Chevalier, Tracy. Dutton, 1999. ISBN: 052594527X. **HIST, ALEX**

Who posed for the Dutch artist Vermeer's celebrated portrait *Girl with a Pearl Earring*? In her enormously popular novel of the same title, Chevalier suggests it was a 16-year-old servant in the artist's seventeenth-century household. The author names her Griet and imaginatively creates a coming-of-age story for her while also offering an intriguing look at the artist's household. The book has been widely (and justifiably) praised for its splendid evocation of daily life in seventeenth-century Holland. A perennially popular crossover novel, it was chosen as a 2000 Alex Award winner.

A second Chevalier novel that will interest YAs is *The Lady and the Unicorn*, which offers a highly romantic look at the making of a set of medieval tapestries known as *The Lady and the Unicorn* sequence. Again, the details of the setting are beautifully realized, and the carefully detailed creation of the tapestries is fascinating stuff. Another winner for Chevalier.

THE GOD OF ANIMALS

Kyle, Aryn. Scribner, 2007. ISBN: 1416533249. **GF, ALEX**

Life is no picnic for 12-year-old Alice. Her mother has been virtually bedridden with depression since the girl's birth; a classmate has just drowned; and her older sister has run off to marry a rodeo cowboy, leaving Alice as her father's principal helper just as the family's horse ranch is struggling to survive both declining business and the hottest summer to hit Desert Valley, Colorado, in fifteen years. Obviously bad things do happen to good people, and Alice and her family certainly seem to be harvesting a bumper crop of badness over the course of this accomplished first novel. Accordingly, readers in search of rainbows and unicorns are advised to steer clear of this work of dark realism. However, those who enjoy character driven fiction, beautifully realized western settings, and the world of horses will find much to appreciate here.

THE HEADMASTER RITUAL

Antrim, Taylor. Houghton Mifflin, 2007. ISBN: 9780618756827. **GF**

The prep school—whether British or American—has always provided a setting ready-made for satire and awkward coming-of-age experiences. The academy this time—the tony Britton School—is an American one and the coming-of-ager is poor James, whose father is the ferociously left-wing headmaster Edward Wolfe, who is much given to wearing Mao jackets and (figuratively) pledging allegiance to Communist North Korea. Into this uneasy mix comes a young history teacher Dyer Martin, whose life will become bound up with James's when Wolfe instructs him to set up a model United Nations. Things are not as they seem to be (are they ever?), and Dyer soon finds himself in a fix, while James finds himself the object of some nasty hazing. Journalist Antrim attended Andover, to which the Britton School bears more than a passing resemblance, and there is no question that the author knows his territory and uses it to good comedic effect.

Though much more serious, another excellent prep school novel profiled in this book is Tobias Wolff's *Old School*.

HIGH FIDELITY

Hornby, Nick. Riverhead, 1995. ISBN: 1573220167. **GF, HUM**

Though many teens will be more familiar with the 2000 film version of this title starring John Cusack, Jack Black, and Catherine Zeta-Jones, British journalist Hornby's first novel is not to be missed. The story of a 30-something vintage record store owner named Rob, the novel charts the course of his life following his abandonment by his live-in girlfriend, Laura. For diversion he tries to rearrange his huge record collection and compile top five lists of everything under the sun (top five episodes of *Cheers*, top five best songs to play at a funeral, top five most memorable split-ups, etc.) with the help of his two store clerks, who provide comic relief. Just when Rob thinks he has his new life under control, he sees Laura again . . .

A best seller in England, where it was first published, the novel travels well to this country, where it succeeds in presenting an offbeat but universally entertaining love story from the point of view of a man. Equally diverting is the clever and often satirical look at the lives and opinions of musical snobs. *Booklist* called this "an amazingly accomplished first novel." Hornby's first novel for teen readers, *Slam*, about a 15-year-old skateboarder who also has girlfriend troubles, is another delightful (okay, amazingly accomplished) read.

THE HISTORIAN

Kostova, Elizabeth. Little, Brown, 2005. ISBN: 0316011770. **SPEC**

The discovery by a motherless 16-year-old girl of a strange medieval book and a packet of letters in her scholar father's library is the catalyst for an epic quest in search of the true history of Vlad Tepes, aka Vlad the Impaler, better known to history as . . . *Drakulya*! The subsequent quest will take the previously sheltered girl not only into the history of the legend but also into the history of her own family and that of her historian father's mentor, Bartholomew Rossi. What will she learn—and will it confirm or disprove the validity of Dracula's own assertion, "History has taught us that the nature of man is evil, sublimely so"? It reportedly took Kostova ten years to write *The Historian*; considering its great length (656 pages), non–vampire fans may claim it'll take that long to read it! Nevertheless, surely its popularity is further illustrated by the fact that it was, in its time, the only first novel to have debuted on the *New York Times* best-seller list at number one, going on to sell more than 1.5 million copies. Kostova's second novel, *The Swan Thieves*, published in 2010, tells the romantic story of a deeply troubled painter and a mystery surrounding a French Impressionist artist.

HOW ALL THIS STARTED
Fromm, Pete. Picador, 2000. ISBN: 0312209339. **GF**

In his well-received first novel Fromm, a prolific short story writer (more than a hundred published), tells how—well—all this started; that is, how 15-year-old Austin and his 20-year-old college dropout sister Abilene (yes, they're named for the cities in which they were conceived) have wound up with their parents in a small Texas town in the middle of nowhere (that actually means the West Texas desert). Austin is a promising pitcher, and his sometimes manic sister—a fine pitcher herself—has decided that she will make him a great one; to that end she devotes her considerable energy to training him. Austin is absolutely devoted to his sister, and it accordingly takes him quite a while to recognize that her whiplash mood swings are signs of a bipolar disorder, one that ultimately cannot go untreated. What this will mean to their close and loving relationship and to Austin's hopes for a baseball career provides the conflict that drives the plot of this extremely fine, character-driven novel, a natural read for baseball fans.

HUGE
Fuerst, James W. Crown, 2009. ISBN: 9780307452498. **HUM, M/S**

Eugene "Huge" Smalls, a 12-year-old with anger management issues, is the protagonist of this engagingly offbeat first novel. Anything but huge, he's frustratingly tiny for his age but nevertheless large in his ambitions. For when an act of vandalism shatters the peace at his beloved grandmother's retirement home, Huge decides to find the perp. Though set in New Jersey in the

1980s, the novel recalls an earlier period when hard-boiled detectives like Philip Marlowe and the Continental Op roamed mean streets on both coasts in search of bad guys. Though Huge dotes on such hard-boiled private dicks from the '30s he is—let's face it—not in their league, and as a result all sorts of hilarious misadventures, misapprehensions, and mishaps occur. As much coming-of-age story as mystery, the novel offers in the person of Huge a hero who commands a large place in the reader's affection and imagination. Though an academic, author Fuerst, who holds a PhD from Harvard and an MFA from The New School, writes accessible and thoroughly delightful fiction. Please, sir, may we have more?

I LOVE YOU, BETH COOPER

Doyle, Larry. HarperCollins, 2007. ISBN: 0061236179. **GF, HUM**

Nerdy high school senior Denis Coverman interrupts his valedictory address at commencement to blurt out his true feelings: "Beth Cooper," he declares, "I love you." Now, Beth, the object of Denis's unrequited passion, is the school's hot-hot-hot chief cheerleader who is—by high school reckoning—light years out of Denis's league. But to his amazement she doesn't have a fainting spell at Denis's news and even shows up at his graduation party. Wow! Unfortunately her army boyfriend Kevin, home on leave, doesn't share her tender feelings and is, in fact, enraged by Denis's declaration, coming after him like an angry freight train. The kinds of complications that ensue are suggested by the fact that Doyle has written for the TV shows *Beavis and Butthead* and *The Simpsons*. Not only does this inspire outrageous incidents, it also lends the book a swift-paced cinematic quality that is sure to delight YAs. Doyle's second novel, *Go Mutants*, is a witty takeoff on teen horror movies that will interest YAs who enjoy *I Love You, Beth Cooper*.

IMANI ALL MINE

Porter, Connie. Houghton Mifflin, 1999. ISBN: 0395838088. **GF, LOI**

Porter's protagonist is a 15-year-old African American girl named Tasha, an honors student, a rape victim, and the single mother of a daughter she has named Imani, which means "faith." The name could well symbolize Tasha's faith in her ability to raise her daughter very much on her own. Set in the inner city of Buffalo, New York, this powerful novel is told in Tasha's voice, which is rich in street dialect and adds significantly to the reader's understanding of her character and motivations. The neighborhood in which she raises her infant daughter is rife with drugs and gang violence, and it is the latter that will lead to a heartbreaking tragedy that will test Tasha's faith. Porter, who is the author of the Addy titles in the American Girl series, has obviously written an entirely different work of fiction here, one that establishes her credentials as an abundantly talented writer of visceral, powerfully immediate, realistic fiction.

IN THE TIME OF THE BUTTERFLIES

Alvarez, Julia. Algonquin Books, 1994. ISBN: 1565120388. **HIST, LOI**

The "butterflies" of the title are the three beautiful Mirabal sisters, Minerva, Patria, and María Teresa, well known for their opposition to the Dominican Republic dictator General Rafael Trujillo. Set in 1960 during the last days of Trujillo's reign, the novel—a fictionalized account of real history—begins with the assassination of the three sisters and proceeds to tell the stories of their lives retrospectively in their own voices. A fourth voice, that of the one surviving sister, Dedé, adds a contemporary account. Vivid and visceral, the voices create a compelling picture of life under a dictatorship and the revolutionary struggle for freedom. For their part in this struggle the sisters have become national heroes in the Dominican Republic, the term *butterflies* being a translation of their underground code name, Las Mariposas.

Alvarez, who has become a well-known author of young adult fiction, says in her story, "A novel is not, after all, a historical document but a way to travel through the human heart." If it is, *In the Time of the Butterflies* provides a moving and memorable journey.

INDECISION

Kunkel, Benjamin. Random House, 2005. ISBN: 1400063450. **GF, HUM**

Literary critic Kunkel's first novel introduces readers both to his 28-year-old protagonist Dwight Wilmerding and also to the (fictional) illness that plagues him: *abulia*, the chronic postcollegiate inability to make up one's mind. Some readers may think this is not an illness but simply a condition of being a Gen Xer; but that aside, Kunkel's conceit is that it is indeed an illness, and one that may finally be curable, thanks to the marvels of modern medicine. In fact, Dwight works for the pharmaceutical giant Pfizer, so he is no stranger to this idea. When his med student roommate suggests he sign up for a trial of a new drug called Abulinix, Dwight is quick to comply. Unfortunately, he is then—as one reviewer waggishly put it—"pfired from Pfizer." But, oh, well, it's as good a reason as any to head off to Quito, Ecuador, to look up a beautiful former classmate named Natasha. There are some very funny scenes in Kunkel's novel and some well-handled meditations on post-9/11 New York, but perhaps Kunkel's main purpose is to inspire his readers to consider indecision in the context of free will and of even freer use of pharmaceuticals.

INTO THE BEAUTIFUL NORTH

Urrea, Luis Alberto. Little, Brown, 2008. ISBN: 9780316025270. **HUM, LOI**

Art imitates life—well, almost—in this sweet-spirited, good-natured story of a Mexican village, Tres Camarones, that has lost almost all of its men to El Norte. In their absence a motley band of gangsters threatens to take over. Feisty 19-year-old Nayeli—who divides her time between working as a waitress in the local café, La Mano Caída, and serving as the campaign manager for her Aunt Irma, a champion bowler, who is running for mayor—is determined to see that doesn't happen. Seeing a screening of *The Magnificent Seven* at the local movie theater (this is where the "art" comes in), Nayeli decides to head north in search of her own magnificent seven who could return with her to Tres Camarones and take care of the incipient bandido problem. And if she happens to find her father, whose last known whereabouts were Kankakee, Illinois, that would be all right, too. So off she goes along with her two best friends, Yolo and Vampi. Tacho, the gay owner of the café, decides to go too. How they manage to get across the Mexican/U.S. border and what happens to them on the other side makes for a delightful and diverting picaresque novel by a popular Latino author who is the winner of both an American Book Award and a Christopher Award.

JAMRACH'S MENAGERIE

Birch, Carol. Doubleday, 2011. ISBN: 9780385534406. **HIST, ADV**

"I was born twice," protagonist Jaffy tells us, "first in a wooden room that jutted out over the black water of the Thames and then again eight years later . . .

when the tiger took me in his mouth." It's this second "birth" that will change the life of the nineteenth-century London street urchin, for the tiger is the property of Mr. Jamrach, an importer of exotic animals, who is so relieved by Jaffy's escape from the animal's jaws that he gives the boy a job. Seven years later he gives Jaffy and his now best friend Tim another assignment: to sail to the South Seas and capture a legendary dragon to sell to an eccentric collector. Adventure quickly turns to misadventure as their ship encounters a horrendous storm, and the book then becomes an almost unbearably suspenseful story of survival. Though Jamrach was a real historical personage who sold animals to P. T. Barnum and the shipwreck is loosely based on the wreck of the whaling ship *Essex*, Birch makes the story uniquely her own, inventing her unforgettable characters and giving the telling of the tale to Jaffy, who has a marvelous narrative voice. This is absolutely top-notch historical fiction that can be read for pleasure and also used in the classroom. For those who prefer their history as nonfiction, a widely praised account of the *Essex* is Nathaniel Philbrick's *In the Heart of the Sea: The Tragedy of the Whaleship* Essex.

JIM THE BOY

Earley, Tony. Little, Brown, 2000. ISBN: 0316199648. **HIST**

Set in the small town of Aliceville, North Carolina, in 1932, this gentle, genial novel traces the year that the boy Jim turns 10. Though his father died a week before he was born and his mother—still grieving—has never remarried, Jim finds male role models in his three bachelor uncles. Together the uncles—Zeno, Coran, and Al—manage the family's rural businesses and farms while at the same time providing love, support, and guidance to Jim during his coming-of-age year. Told in the form of interrelated stories that smoothly cohere, the book is a beautifully written salute to the past while at the same time a celebration of the universal experience of being young. This charming novel, with its multigenerational appeal, will remind some readers of *Dandelion Wine*, Ray Bradbury's similarly wonderful episodic novel of growing up in small-town America. A professor at Vanderbilt University in Nashville, Earley was named one of the twenty best young American fiction writers of 1996 by *Granta* magazine. In 2008 he wrote a sequel of sorts to *Jim the Boy*. Titled *The Blue Star*, it is set on the eve of World War II and tells the evocative story of how Jim—now a high school senior—falls in love for the first time.

JPOD

Coupland, Douglas. Bloomsbury, 2007. ISBN: 9781596911055. **HUM**

Coupland's novel *Generation X* helped define a whole generation of Americans; in this novel he continues his cutting-edge ways, examining the lives of a group of geeks working together on development in a Vancouver video game corporation. Our hero, Ethan Jarlewski (the surname of everyone he works with begins with *J*), lives a surreal life at work and at home, where his mother is a marijuana farmer, his father a would-be actor, and his brother—well, he has stashed twenty illegal Chinese immigrants in Ethan's apartment. And, oh yes, in a nicely metafictional twist, Coupland himself is a character in this extravaganza. In other words, don't expect a smooth narrative ride from Coupland's latest satirical laugh-fest; just fasten your seatbelt and enjoy the bumpy ride.

THE KITCHEN GOD'S WIFE

Tan, Amy. Putnam, 1991. ISBN: 0399135782. **GF, LOI**

Tan's celebrated first novel, *The Joy Luck Club*, was published in 1989, missing the chronological parameters of this book by a single year. Happily, Tan's equally successful second novel made the cut. Like the first, it is a penetrating look at the relationship of mother and daughter. The story is largely that of the mother, Winnie, who tells her adult, American-born daughter, Pearl, the whole story of her youth in China in the 1940s, her abandonment by her own mother, the difficulties of her arranged marriage, the horrors of World War II and the Japanese invasion, and more. How Winnie survived all of this is, it becomes clear, due to the support and love of her female friends. The revelations create a new bond between Winnie and Pearl that is deeply satisfying to both them and to the reader.

THE KITE RUNNER

Hosseini, Khaled. Riverhead, 2003. ISBN: 1573222453. **GF, LOI, ALEX**

As the U.S. war in Afghanistan enters its second decade, this novel set there in the 1970s remains timely and apposite. It is the story of the unlikely friendship of two motherless boys: Amir, the son of a wealthy merchant, and Hassan, the son of one of the family's servants. The relationship, though close, is uneven for reasons other than class and caste. Hassan worships Amir, but the wealthy, insecure boy is jealous of his father's obvious affection for the servant boy. When Amir discovers Hassan being raped by a gang of neighborhood boys, he refuses to intervene and, overcome by guilt, then conspires to have Hassan and his father expelled from the household. Out of sight, out of mind? Not exactly. When the Soviets subsequently invade, Amir and his father escape to America. Years later, the now-adult Amir is given a chance to redeem himself, though it means returning to Afghanistan, now under Taliban control. An Afghani American doctor living in the San Francisco Bay Area, Hosseini demonstrates in his debut novel a true gift for characterization, a love for his native country, and a deep appreciation of its culture and politics.

In his subsequent novel, *A Thousand Splendid Suns*, the author views thirty years of Afghanistan's recent history through the eyes of two women: Mariam is the illegitimate daughter of a maid, while Laila is the daughter of liberal, educated parents. Unlike Amir and Hassan in *The Kite Runner*, who are peers, Mariam and Laila are separated by a generation, Mariam being the older. As events develop, Mariam and Laila assume a mother-daughter relationship that becomes especially important when the Russians are expelled and the ascendant Taliban takes over, imposing a regime of violence and repression. Much darker than *The Kite Runner*, *A Thousand Splendid Suns* is not without its tragic elements; but, as before, Hosseini's intimate knowledge of Afghanistan and its people make for a compelling and rewarding reading experience.

LAMB

Moore, Christopher. Morrow, 2002. ISBN: 0380978407. **SPEC, HUM**

Jesus didn't really have a best friend named Biff—but what, author Moore wonders, if he did, and what if Biff were to be brought back to life to recount Jesus's first thirty years of life? The result is often irreverent (no surprise there) but just as often humorous and intriguing. A central part of the story is Biff's account of the trip the two young men take to India in search of the three wise men who brought gifts to the infant Joshua, as Jesus is called here. The two also hope to find wisdom about Joshua's identity and his destiny. There are abundant opportunities here for satire—all of which Biff takes—but the story assumes a more serious tone when the two return home and Moore deals with the traditional story of Jesus's work and death. Clearly not for every reader and sure to offend many, the novel has nevertheless been a great favorite of teens who enjoy its irreverence and occasional laugh-out-loud lines. To his credit, Moore also does an excellent job of recreating his historic milieu.

A LESSON BEFORE DYING

Gaines, Ernest J. Knopf, 1993. ISBN: 0679414770. **HIST, LOI**

Gaines's novel is another classic example of an adult novel for YAs. Set in small-town Louisiana in 1948, a time when racial discrimination is still a rampant way of life, a young black man named Jefferson is wrongfully accused of complicity in the murder of a white man. Despite the injustice of the charge, it's nevertheless inevitable—because of the nature of the crime—that he will be executed. His white defense attorney regards him as little more than an animal, and it's clear that Jefferson himself feels no sense of self-worth. However, his godmother, Miss Emma, is determined that he will die with dignity and persuades Grant Wiggins, the teacher at the local black school, to counsel her godson. But who needs the counseling more? Grant himself has grown up on the local plantation and accordingly struggles with his own self-image. However, as he and Jefferson work together, both gradually come to value their individuality and experience new feelings of dignity. There's no traditional happy ending to this moving novel but one that celebrates the dignity and worth of each individual. In certain details of plot and theme, Gaines's novel may remind contemporary YA readers of Walter Dean Myers's Printz Award–winning YA novel *Monster*. Gaines is also the author of another modern classic of African American literature, *The Autobiography of Miss Jane Pittman*.

LIFE OF PI

Martel, Yann. Harcourt, 2001. ISBN: 0151008116. **SPEC**

Along with *The Curious Incident of the Dog in the Night-Time*, Martel's novel was one of the first to usher in the modern trend in crossover novels—that is, books published as either adult or young adult titles that appeal to both generations of readers. Just as it has multiple readerships, so it has multiple layers of meaning. But it is the confoundingly original premise that will hook readers and not let their attention go until the final page. Here's the story: when the ship carrying Pi Patel from India to Canada sinks, the teenage boy finds himself stranded in a lifeboat with a 450-pound Bengal tiger named Richard Parker! How the two survive for 227 lost-at-sea days makes for page-turning suspense and laugh-out-loud humor. It also makes for an increasingly serious philosophical novel that explores—though never oppressively so—questions about the nature of humankind and of God. And since there are no definitive answers to *those* questions, so there is no definitive conclusion to Canadian writer Martel's mind-teasing fiction. In a novel about belief, it's altogether appropriate to wonder if one can believe that Pi is a reliable narrator. Did things happen as he states them? Or did his ordeal at sea somehow scramble his wits and lead to a delusional mindset? Readers are invited to make up their own minds, a fact that will frustrate some but will delight others. Regardless, Martel's masterful storytelling abilities will surely stick in all their memories.

THE LITTLE FRIEND

Tartt, Donna. Knopf, 2001. ISBN: 0679439382. **M/S**

The *New York Times Book Review* noted this "might be described as a young-adult novel for adults," a description that was meant as a compliment, since, the staid *Times* added, "it can carry us back to the breathless state of adolescent literary discovery." What readers will discover here—breathless or not—is a very long (six-hundred-plus pages) and complex literary mystery. Set in small-town Mississippi in the 1970s, this is the story of how 12-year-old Harriet Dufresnes sets about solving the murder—nine years previously—of her then 9-year-old brother, Robin. Her snap decision is that the murderer was a local good-for-nothing redneck named Danny Ratliff (the name is probably a reference to a William Faulkner character named V. K. Ratliff). Now all she has to do is prove it, aided only by Hely, an adoring (boy) friend. The book is filled with eccentric characters, including Harriet's four maiden aunts, who fill her in on her family's sometimes checkered past. The atmosphere is pure Southern gothic, which evokes not only the spirit of William Faulkner but also of Flannery O'Connor and Harper Lee. Higher praise cannot be offered! Readers of this will also want to check out Tartt's acclaimed first novel, *The Secret History*, also featuring a cast of eccentrics and a murder but set at a small liberal arts college in Vermont. That story is as cerebral as its setting.

LOCAS

Hernandez, Jaime. Fantagraphics, 2004. ISBN: 156097611X. **GN, LOI**

With his brothers Gilbert and Mario, Hernandez created the longstand-ing comics series Love and Rockets, but these stories—collected from that source—are completely his own and represent a significant contribution to twentieth-century graphic art. Maggie is a young Mexican American woman living in Los Angeles in the 1980s. Attracted to the emerging punk scene, she meets Hopey, a rabid punkette, and the two become friends. These sto-ries chart that friendship while also offering an in-depth look at Chicana working-class life and culture. Hernandez pulls no punches in the unsparing realism he brings to the stories, including the sexual lives of the two young women. Additionally, these stories are extraordinary exercises in visual nar-rative art that are further enhanced by the richness of their characterizations.

THE LOVELY BONES

Sebold, Alice. Little, Brown, 2002. ISBN: 0316666343. **SPEC**

Really, what is left to say about this book that hasn't already been said? A huge best seller that was made into a movie, it has excited widespread discus-sion—and a host of imitators—because of its unusual premise: its protagonist, 14-year-old Susie Salmon, who tells the story in her own first-person voice, is dead, murdered on her way home from school. The story she tells from her new home in heaven is essentially one of how her survivors deal with her death and how their lives are changed. There are moments of heartbreak, of course, but also of triumph. In her *Booklist* review, Kristine Huntley wrote that Sebold "brings the novel to a conclusion that is unfalteringly magnificent."

THE MAGICIANS

Grossman, Lev. Viking, 2009. ISBN: 9780670020553. **SPEC, ALEX**

Grossman's novel of dark magic will remind many readers of Hogwarts, but with alcohol and sex. High school senior Quentin, who has always been fas-cinated by a series of children's fantasies about a magical land called Fillory, finds himself improbably enrolled at Brakebills College for Magical Pedagogy in upstate New York. Alas, learning magic is no guarantee of happiness, and following graduation, Quentin finds himself leading an aimless, purposeless life until (wait for it) he discovers that Fillory is a real place! But, once again, the reality is different—and far more dangerous—than the fantasy. A sequel has now been published: *The Magician King*. In this one Quentin goes on a quest to find seven gold keys and gets more than he bargained for. In the meantime readers learn the back story of Queen Julia, the "witch queen."

Grossman is not only an accomplished fantasist but also the book critic for *Time* magazine. Readers who enjoy *The Magicians* may want to ferret out his first novel, *Codex*, a bibliothriller involving an ancient codex and a modern online computer game that may be more than it first appears to be.

MARY REILLY

Martin, Valerie. Doubleday, 1990. ISBN: 0385249683. **HOR, HIST**

Martin's imaginative retelling of Robert Louis Stevenson's classic *Strange Case of Dr. Jekyll and Mr. Hyde* is presented from the perspective and told in the vernacular voice of Jekyll's maidservant, Mary Reilly. The result is not only suspenseful and true to its original source, but also richly atmospheric as Martin recreates a Victorian London that rivals the Sherlock Holmes stories in its verisimilitude. Readers who enjoy *Mary Reilly* will want to look at the similar recasting *Jekyll, Alias Hyde* by Donald Thomas. In a nice twist, Thomas is also the author of a number of Sherlock Holmes pastiches.

THE MEANING OF CONSUELO

Cofer, Judith Ortiz. Farrar Straus Giroux, 2003. ISBN: 0374205094. **HIST, LOI**

Set in 1950s Puerto Rico, Cofer's novel is the story of the eponymous Consuelo, an intelligent, bookish girl who is charged with caring for her sister Mili (short for *milagros*, or *miracle*), who is emotionally troubled and may be headed for full-scale psychosis. Meanwhile Puerto Rican life and culture are changing, a process reflected in Consuelo's home life, which is dominated by her parents' incessant quarreling over her father's fascination with all things American and her mother's equal commitment to traditional Puerto Rican life and culture. Lost somewhere in the middle is Consuelo, whose struggle to discover her own identity reflects the larger struggle of her homeland.

MISS NEW INDIA

Mukherjee, Bharati. Houghton Mifflin Harcourt, 2011. ISBN: 9780618646531. **GF, LOI**

The titular new Miss India is teenager Anjali Bose, who flees her village and an arranged marriage. On the advice of her American expat teacher she heads for the city of Bangalore, the center of India's burgeoning cyberculture. There she hopes to find a job working as a service agent at a call center (any American who has ever made a phone call for technical support or billing questions or even dinner reservations will be familiar with the sound of an Indian voice answering the phone). Angie's evolution from naive small-town girl to urban wannabe sophisticate mirrors the transformation of India itself. And as the Indian subcontinent becomes a major world power, a host of writers like Mukherjee are giving faces to young Indians whose lives are becoming ever more Americanized. This is not only an excellent novel but an important book for all young people who are interested in our rapidly changing world.

MISTER PIP

Jones, Lloyd. Dial, 2007. ISBN: 9780385341066. **GF, LOI, ALEX**

To a remote island off the coast of New Guinea comes an eccentric Englishman who assumes the de facto role of teacher to twenty young people there. His text for teaching is Dickens's *Great Expectations*, and so connected is he in his students' minds to the work that he soon becomes known as Mr. Pip. The island is hardly a paradise, alas, and several different kinds of conflict soon emerge. One involves the mother of the teacher's star pupil, 13-year-old Matilda, for the parent fears the teacher will destroy the local culture through his stories of life in England and is determined to do something about it. A much more serious conflict, however, derives from a local war that is raging and that will bring violence to the village, which provides the story's setting. The parallels between narrator Matilda's coming-of-age and the Dickens novel are nicely and unobtrusively handled. As a result, it is altogether a splendid novel that has in the few short years since its publication become a great favorite of YA readers. Author Jones knows his territory very well, having been born in New Zealand, where he continues to live with his wife. This is his eighth novel.

MONTANA 1948

Watson, Larry. Milkweed Editions, 1993. ISBN: 0915943131. **HIST**

Narrator David Hayden recalls the terrible summer of 1948 when he was 12 and his family was ripped apart. How so? It begins when his father, the local sheriff, has no choice but to arrest his older brother, a war hero and the town doctor, for committing serial rapes of Sioux Indian women in his care. This truth is revealed when the Haydens' housekeeper adamantly refuses to see Dr. Hayden when she falls grievously ill. When she subsequently dies, David gives evidence that implicates his uncle. To spare his brother the embarrassment of being publicly jailed, David's father then locks Dr. Hayden in the family's basement, where he subsequently commits suicide. Clearly there are tragic overtones to this beautifully written coming-of-age novel, but its power makes it unforgettable, and its exquisite treatment of its setting—the landscape of Mercer County, Montana—is a tour de force, as is its demonstration of the inescapable link between character and context.

MORE LIKE NOT RUNNING AWAY

Shepherd, Paul. Sarabande Books, 2006. ISBN: 1932511288. **GF**

Twelve-year-old Levi adores his carpenter father even though the man, restless and angry, moves his family constantly, almost as if he were running away. Levi's circumstances routinely change accordingly; what remains always the same are the voices he hears and has heard his whole life. Sometimes they sound like God, and sometimes they sound so much like his father that it's hard to distinguish between the two. But as his father's behavior becomes more erratic and possibly dangerous, it's the redemption of silence that Levi seeks. This powerful father and son story, Shepherd's first novel, won the 2004 Mary McCarthy Prize in Short Fiction, selected by Larry Woiwode, who in his introduction calls *More Like Not Running Away* "haunting" and praises its "surefooted forward momentum." Also praiseworthy is the spot-on first-person voice that Shepherd has given Levi, his narrator. "The air tasted green like after rain," the boy tells us. "A voice, soft and canyon deep, vibrated in the bones of my head." And it is Levi's voice, soft and deep, quiet but reverberant, that will remain with the reader long after the other voices have faded.

MY NEW AMERICAN LIFE

Prose, Francine. HarperCollins, 2011. ISBN: 9780061713767. **GF, LOI**

Prose is not only a critic (see her entry in the nonfiction section) but also a fine novelist. Here is the proof of it in her latest work of fiction, the story of Lula, a 26-year-old emigrant from Albania, who is working as a nanny in New Jersey. Amusingly enough, her charge is a bored teenager, Zeke, who is old enough to be in college (his single-parent father doesn't want him home alone)! The book's conceit is that this is Lula's diary, an account she has been encouraged to write by her immigration lawyer, Don. The diary is often wildly funny in its perceptions of her new homeland, but things become really interesting when three Albanian criminals show up on the doorstep with an unusual request. In addition to its page-turning story, Prose's latest also offers an intimate portrait of some of the universal experiences of recent immigrants to the United States.

Older YAs may also like Prose's *Blue Angel*. It tells the often funny, occasionally fraught story of a university creative writing teacher into whose class comes a funky but desirable young student named Angela Argo—and before you can say "sexual harassment," the teacher, Ted Swenson, finds himself in potentially serious trouble. Clearly inspired by the Marlene Dietrich/Josef von Sternberg movie of the same title, this happy combination will invite some creative writing exercises of its own . . .

NEVER LET ME GO

Ishiguro, Kazuo. Knopf, 2005. ISBN: 1400043395. **SPEC, ALEX**

When two of her childhood best friends and classmates reenter her life, 31-year-old Kathy recalls for the reader their often halcyon student years together at the exclusive, secluded—and mysterious—Hailsham School. While encouraged to develop their own intellectual and artistic abilities and interests, the students there are constantly reminded that they are "special," and so they are—but it will take the reader some time to realize why: they're clones being raised for the harvesting of their body parts. This is to be done according to a carefully controlled schedule, including a term as a "carer" like Kathy before they begin their cycle of organ donations. Ishiguro offers his readers an accessible but never simplistic story that involves wide-ranging questions about the meaning of being human and the ethicality of compromising and disturbing that essential meaning. The critics have been unanimous in calling *Never Let Me Go* Ishiguro's finest novel since his Booker Prize–winning *The Remains of the Day*. Readers interested in another fine novel about human cloning might want to have a look at *The Bradbury Report* by Steven Polansky.

NINETEEN MINUTES

Picoult, Jodi. Atria, 2007. ISBN: 9780743496728. **GF, ALEX**

Picoult is among the most popular authors of adult books for YAs in part, perhaps, because her issue-driven novels reflect the real-life experiences of today's teens. In her fourteenth novel, for example, she tells the urgently important and deeply felt story of teen violence in a small New Hampshire town. With echoes of Columbine, the story tells how Peter Houghton, an abused and bullied 17-year-old, brings a gun to high school and opens fire, killing nine of his classmates and a teacher in nineteen minutes. How could this happen? What part did the community play and what guilt must it—and Peter's clueless parents—bear? These questions are dealt with in the searing account of the trial that follows and that also tells the story of the relationship between the presiding judge, Alex Cormier, and her daughter Josie, whose boyfriend has been one of the chief bullies. As noted above, Picoult specializes in writing fiction based on ripped-from-the-headlines incidents, and she has written here a combination thriller and work of social comment, a type of novel that the late Robert Cormier wrote so effectively. Could the judge's name be a tribute to him?

My Sister's Keeper is another Picoult novel featuring a court case. This one is the story of 13-year-old Anna Fitzgerald who sues her parents—for the rights to her own body. She has been asked to donate a kidney to her older sister, who suffers from leukemia. Anna loves her sister and has already donated bone marrow and blood, but this time she doesn't want to do the procedure. Will it tear her family apart? Readers will be anxious to find out.

OLD SCHOOL

Wolff, Tobias. Knopf, 2003. ISBN: 0375401466. **GF**

Author of the classic coming-of-age memoir *This Boy's Life* and a host of short stories, Wolff has now written his first novel. Set in 1960 at an elite New

England prep school, this is the story of an unnamed narrator/protagonist, a scholarship student and outsider who longs to become a writer. When it is announced that Ernest Hemingway, no less, will visit the campus and will meet with the winner of a writing competition, the narrator is determined to win—so determined that he "borrows" an idea and reveals a family secret, with devastating consequences. Wolff, who teaches at Stanford University, has a great deal of interest to say about writing, while imagined visits to the school by both an aged Robert Frost and a fire-breathing Ayn Rand offer wonderful opportunities for satire. Readers of this novel may wish to also read Taylor Antrim's *The Headmaster Ritual.* More important, they won't want to miss Wolff's compelling memoir *This Boy's Life.*

THE OUTSIDE BOY

Cummins, Jeanine. New American Library, 2010. ISBN: 9780451229489. **GF, LOI**

When 12-year-old Christy's beloved Grandda dies, not only does a human being pass on, but so perhaps may a whole way of life. For Christy is an Irish Traveler, a Pavee, and though the world no longer calls him and his family Gypsies, their way of life remains largely unchanged as they travel in caravans from town to town with no fixed place to call home. But it's 1959 and times are changing, and with the death of their paterfamilias and the emergence of long-held secrets, Christy's family may have to change with them. Cummins is clearly sympathetic to the often vilified Pavee but is nevertheless quite candid in her depiction of their occasional petty thefts and tradition of mooching. *The Outside Boy* is a marvel of Irish storytelling further enhanced by the wonderfully vernacular first-person narrative voice Cummins has created for young Christy. His poignant but often funny story of his larger-than-life family is enriched by its implicit expression of the book's theme: the quest for a place to belong and for people with whom to share it.

OVER AND UNDER

Tucker, Todd. St. Martin's, 2008. ISBN: 9780312379902. **HIST, ALEX**

Thomas Jefferson and Andrew Jackson are best friends. No, not the former presidents. This Jefferson and Jackson are surnamed Kruer and Gray, respectively, and they are 14-year-old best friends living in a small town in southern Indiana. It's the summer of 1979, and the boys' friendship is about to be tested. The catalyst for this is a strike at the Borden Casket Company, where their fathers work: Tom's is labor and Andy's is management—and therein lies the rub. In the meantime Tom's cousin gets involved in some dangerous business, and it appears that Andy's mom and the handsome local sheriff have a—well, call it *dubious* secret. There is enough drama, in short, to keep the pages turning while an air of sweet but never stifling nostalgia hangs over the entire work. Tom and Andy are feisty and funny and, as I said in my starred *Booklist* review, "as likable as Labrador retriever pups."

THE PARTICULAR SADNESS OF LEMON CAKE

Bender, Aimee. Doubleday, 2010. ISBN: 9780385501125. **GF, SPEC, ALEX**

On her ninth birthday Rose Edelstein discovers she has a strange gift—the ability to taste other people's emotions in the food they prepare. As she grows up, she learns that what began as a gift may be turning into a curse, one that has been shared by other members of her family. How we cope with emotions plays a large thematic role in this small but deeply felt novel that focuses not only on Rose but also on her relatives. Bender's previous novel, *The Girl in the Flammable Skirt*, has been described as surrealistic, but this one is rooted in a more accessible magical realism. In fact, the novel was selected as a 2011 Alex Award winner—one of the top ten adult novels of the year for young adults.

THE PERKS OF BEING A WALLFLOWER

Chbosky, Stephen. MTV/Pocket Books, 1999. ISBN: 0671027344. **GF, LOI**

Set in 1991, this epistolary novel is told in the form of letters, from 15-year-old high school freshman Charlie to an anonymous recipient the boy has heard is a nice person. Many readers may feel the letters are addressed to them as Charlie writes about his personal disaffection and the problems he has experienced since a friend of his committed suicide in middle school. Charlie is helped by an understanding English teacher, but his real healing begins when he meets stepsiblings Samantha and Patrick, who are seniors. Together they take the boy under their wing and give him the understanding, affection, and support he urgently needs. Charlie returns a measure of this support when he learns that Patrick is gay. Though he is straight himself, he says to Patrick, who is suffering from the abrupt ending of a relationship, "You know, Patrick? If I were gay, I'd want to date you." The novel helped launch the MTV imprint of adult crossover books. In the years since, the book has become something of a modern cult classic and has seldom been out of the news, since it remains a fixture of ALA's list of most often challenged books. It is not possible to convey the extraordinary quality of innocence that this book emanates along with a tone that perfectly captures Charlie's mood as he grows from hurt to healing. The only way to do justice to this marvelous book is to read it.

PIGEON ENGLISH

Kelman, Stephen. Houghton Mifflin Harcourt, 2011. ISBN: 9780547500607. **GF, LOI**

Set in contemporary London, this is the haunting story of an immigrant family from Ghana that is told through the eyes of 11-year-old Harrison. Surrounded by pimps, prostitutes, poverty, drug abuse, and gang warfare, the family's life is a daily struggle. But nothing can dampen Harrison's cheerful attitude toward life—not even the murder of a neighborhood boy who has been kind to him. True, death is always present in life; however, Harrison doesn't see this as an opportunity to philosophize but, rather, to turn detective, hoping—with the help of his friend Dean—to solve the case and collect the reward he imagines will be forthcoming. Of course, 11-year-olds don't always fully understand what they see around them, and Harrison and Dean may encounter more than they have bargained for. This first novel reflects the author's own early life growing up in the projects. As a result, the setting of his novel and the intimate details of daily life there are strengths of this book, but so is the wonderful first-person vernacular he has created for Harrison. The "pigeon English" of the title, it is this voice that rescues the book from any hint of didacticism and humanizes the universal immigrant experience.

THE PILLARS OF THE EARTH / WORLD WITHOUT END

Follett, Ken. Macmillan, 1989. ISBN: 0333519833 /
Dutton, 2007. ISBN: 9780525950073. **HIST**

The kind of book for which the word *epic* was coined, this two-volume historical blockbuster (nearly two thousand pages long!) is a departure for Follett, a popular writer of suspense fiction, but is nevertheless among his most popular work, and with good reason. The first volume tells the compelling story of the building of a twelfth-century cathedral. The action plays out over a four-decade period during which the cathedral nearly becomes a character in itself, enhanced and enriched by the lives and fortunes of the three men—and three women—who are inextricably connected with it. Thanks to its rich characterizations, its beautifully realized medieval setting, and its grandly sweeping plot, the novel is a compellingly readable epic, as is its sequel, *World without End*, which is set in the same town but two centuries later and features descendants of the characters from *Pillars*. Like the first volume, this is a marvel of verisimilitude that takes the reader into a chronologically remote period and brings it to richly realized life. This one, too, has compelling characters (four main ones in this case) and a riveting, page-turning plot enriched by an intriguing mystery. Historical fiction is said to be a hard sell to teens but this one will sell itself. Readers who might want to know more about cathedrals and their construction won't want to miss David Macaulay's first book, *Cathedral: The Story of Its Construction*. Even better, they should seek out a copy of Macaulay's later title, *Building the Book* Cathedral. As the title suggests, this volume contains not only the original contents but Macaulay's fascinating, richly illustrated examination of the process that went into the book's creation and execution. As for those who want another novel about the building of a cathedral, one can't go wrong with Nobel Laureate William Golding's *The Spire*.

PLAINSONG

Haruf, Kent. Knopf, 1999. ISBN: 0375406182. **GF, ALEX**

Though Haruf's third novel has been compared to the work of both William Faulkner and Flannery O'Connor, it is not set in the South but instead on the high Colorado plains east of Denver, in the small town of Holt. There the story follows the interconnected lives of eight characters. Among the principals is a high school teacher named Tom Guthrie, who is attempting to raise his two young sons, Ike, 10, and Bobby, 9, as a single parent. Meanwhile another teacher, Maggie Jones, has arranged for pregnant teen Victoria Roubideaux—abandoned by her family—to become a boarder with the two elderly McPheron brothers, who may remind some readers of those Norwegian bachelor farmers that Garrison Keillor is always talking about. Certainly the McPherons are a study in social distance, comfortable only with each other and after many years of this, not much for conversation, either. Their interactions with Maggie are at first funny but gradually become touching without being in any way sentimental. As the characters tell their stories in alternating chapters, the novel becomes a celebration of nontraditional families and also boasts a beautifully realized setting that is a kind of love letter to small town and farm life. Altogether, *Plainsong* is the kind of flawless novel that every writer wishes he or she had written, and it inarguably will find its way near the top of any list of the best adult books for YA readers. It's a modern classic.

Five years after the publication of Plainsong, Haruf published a sequel, *Eventide*. This novel finds Victoria and her baby, Katie, leaving their home with the McPheron brothers so Victoria can attend college. Haruf introduces a handful of new characters who continue the story with the same kind of humanity that underscored his first novel. As this second novel seamlessly evolves, the reader will come to realize that what links it to the first—and that what makes both so wonderfully memorable is their rare quality of goodness. Though *Eventide* can be read as a stand-alone novel, readers will find the experience much richer if they have first read *Plainsong*.

THE POE SHADOW

Pearl, Matthew. Random House, 2006. ISBN: 1400061032. **M/S, HIST**

Here is something different, a combination literary/historical/mystery novel involving the eternally popular Edgar Allan Poe—though he wasn't quite so popular in his own day, Pearl claims. This is important, for when Poe dies under mysterious circumstances, his great fan Quentin Hobson Clark, a wealthy young lawyer, is outraged by the callous disregard of the press. Vowing to solve the mystery of Poe's death and restore his reputation, Clark travels to France to enlist the aid of the Frenchman he believes to be the real-life model of Poe's fictitious detective C. Auguste Dupin (who appeared in the Poe short story "The PurLOIned Letter," widely considered to be the first American mystery). Things become complicated when a second claimant to the mantle of inspiration appears and is fit to be tied that Clark has chosen the other. He follows the two to America, where things turn deadly and the plot thickens like my mother's gravy. It's all great fun for both Poe and mystery fans.

Pearl is also the author of a second mystery of this sort, *The Dante Club*. Following two murders of particularly gruesome sorts—the first involves maggots, the second premature burial—a clutch of literary celebrities who are members of the Dante Club (which actually existed in nineteenth-century

Boston, the setting for this novel) resolve to solve the mysteries of the deaths, which they recognize as being inspired by Dante's *Inferno*. *Booklist* hailed this one as "a unique and utterly absorbing tale." Fans of Pearl's mysteries may want to have a look at Caleb Carr's work, too.

THE POISONWOOD BIBLE

Kingsolver, Barbara. HarperFlamingo, 1998. ISBN: 0060995386. **HIST, LOI**

To the Belgian Congo in 1959 come Baptist missionary/evangelist Nathan Price, his wife, and their four daughters. Though the stiff-necked Price clearly regards himself as a patriarchal character, this is less his story than that of his wife and daughters, all of whom take turns narrating. The eldest daughter, solipsistic Rachel, is 16; the youngest, Ruth May, is 5, while twins Leah and Adah fall in between. Kingsolver does a marvelous job of creating individual voices for each of the daughters and for the mother, Orleanna, as well. And a good thing, too, for the story they have to tell approaches the epic, spread over three decades and contemplating the extraordinary—and often tragic—events that visited the transformation of the Congo into Zaire. The author also does rough justice to Price's naive but often dictatorial attempts to impose Christianity on native culture and beliefs, an attempt that ironically mirrors the political turmoil of the time. Readers who are familiar with Kingsolver's earlier work, which is typically set in the American Southwest, may be surprised by this unusual setting, but the author herself lived for a time in the Congo when she was a child and her parents worked there in public health service. Her memories of that experience have clearly served her well in the creation of this extraordinarily ambitious—and successful—work.

PREP

Sittenfeld, Curtis. Random House, 2005. ISBN: 1400062314. **ROM**

Here is an early example of another type of crossover novel: one that, though published as adult, could well have been published for young adults. In the years since, this has become an increasingly common phenomenon. In fact, I have been reviewing this type of book for *Booklist* since this title was published. As I explain in my introduction, it is typically publishers' sales and marketing departments (working sometimes in concert with the Barnes &

Noble retail chain) that make the decision as to whether a title will be published as adult or YA. Frankly, there is a good deal more money to be made from publishing as adult (with the rare exception of the Harry Potter or Twilight books). As for this title, it's a fairly traditional school story set in an exclusive prep school on the East Coast. The protagonist, 17-year-old Lee, is a scholarship student from South Bend, Indiana. Not surprisingly she feels like an outsider—until, that is, the handsomest boy in the school appears in her bedroom one night! Passions are spent, mistakes are made, and Lee is left older but wiser. The novel is smoothly written, and Lee, though tiresomely introspective, is an otherwise interesting character—interesting enough that this title became a huge best seller. Go figure.

PRIDE OF BAGHDAD

Vaughan, Brian K. Art by Niko Henrichon. Vertigo, 2006. ISBN: 1401203140. **GN, GF**

This compelling graphic novel is based on a real incident that took place in 2003 during the Iraq War, when the Baghdad Zoo was bomb damaged and a pride of lions (two females, a male, and a cub) escaped their confines. Told from the lions' perspective—they communicate with one another as in a talking animal story—the city they see is a bleak commentary on the senseless violence of the war as are their encounters with other animals. The mixed and dangerous blessing of the lions' sudden freedom is also clearly intended as a commentary on the war and its impact on the Iraqi people (the lions are killed by U.S. troops). A memorable and haunting story that also demonstrates how Henrichon's beautiful art complements and expands the author's text.

PROJECT X

Shepard, Jim. Knopf, 2004. ISBN: 140004071X. **GF, ALEX**

In the wake of the Columbine shootings, Shepard writes of two disaffected middle-school students, Edwin and Flake, eighth-graders who have been the object of relentless bullying. Edwin ("I'm the kid you think about when you want to make yourself feel better") is the narrator, writing in a flat, affectless voice that nevertheless becomes increasingly vivid as it describes the boys' growing rage and desire for revenge, which result in their planning what they call Project X. Perhaps predictable but also powerful, their attempts to put their plan into action will end badly, if not tragically. *Project X* belongs in every collection of books about teen violence and bullying. Shepard, the author of six novels and four short story collections, teaches creative writing at Williams College.

PYGMY

Palahniuk, Chuck. Doubleday, 2009. ISBN: 9780385526340. **GF, HUM**

Palahniuk has had a cult following since his first novel *Fight Club* (made into a film starring Brad Pitt). In this, uh, *unusual* novel—his tenth—he shows why. Meet 13-year-old Pygmy, a foreign exchange student-cum-terrorist come to America along with a clutch of other kids to implement "Operation Havoc." The story is told in a series of dispatches from Pygmy written in his bizarre form of English that is sometimes hilarious, sometimes incomprehensible; for example,

> Begins here second account of operative me, agent number 67, on arrival retail product distribution facility of city ??. Outlet number ??. Date ??. For official record, during American winter youth attend compulsive levels of teaching; during summer, American youth must attend shopping mall.

The point of all this is social satire that—like Pygmy's tenuous grasp of English—is sometimes funny, sometimes spot-on, sometimes stinging, and sometimes baffling. This is definitely not for every reader, but fans will adore it, especially the fact that it'll give a lot of adult authority figures apoplexy!

Fight Club, the author's first novel and a model of nihilism, established his reputation as a take-no-prisoners champion of disaffected Gen X youth. Thanks to the success of the movie, the novel's conceit is familiar to many readers. They will know that Tyler Durden is the founder of the Fight Club in which young men gather to beat the daylights out of each other, since nobody much cares if they live or die. As this becomes a national movement, disaffection and alienation approach anarchy, which is Durden's goal. Much darker than *Pygmy*, *Fight Club*'s satire is delivered with a bludgeon instead of a wink and a nod. Still, many consider this a brilliant work. YAs and the adults in their lives will make their own judgments.

THE RADLEYS

Haig, Matt. Free Press, 2011. ISBN: 9781439194010. **HOR, ALEX**

"Why are the Radleys so *weird*?" the popular girl at school sneers. Hmmm . . . could it be because they're . . . *vampires*? Why, yes, as a matter of fact, they are. But here's the rub: the two Radley kids—teenagers Rowan and slightly younger sister Clara—don't know it! Thinking it for the best, their abstaining parents—Peter, a doctor, and Helen, an artist—have kept the truth from the children as they, themselves, have refused to indulge their own bloodlust. Not an ideal situation but—though uncomfortable—an honorable one, until the night when Clara, on her way home from a party, is assaulted by a rugby-playing bully from school. When he attempts to rape her, she scratches his face, tastes a drop of his blood, discovers her inner vampire, and tears his throat out. Ooops. In a panic Clara's father calls his older brother, Will—a still-practicing vampire—for help. And the darkly Byronic, deeply charismatic, utterly dissolute Will answers the call. Too bad for the Radleys, for that's when things become a bloody mess; but good for the reader, since that's when the plot kicks into overdrive as complication piles upon complication, keeping one hooked until the very end of this thoroughly compelling, beautifully conceived and executed novel of horror and suspense.

Haig is also the author of a wonderful novel called *The Dead Fathers Club*. When its protagonist, 11-year-old Philip, sees the ghost of his newly dead father, the paternal shade asks the boy to murder his murderer: his own brother. Poor Philip. To kill or not to kill? Yes, the story is cleverly based on Shakespeare's *Hamlet*, and the author hasn't missed a beat in crafting his own version. In the process he has created a wonderful first-person voice for the indecisive Philip. It all makes for great reading fun!

READY PLAYER ONE

Cline, Ernest. Crown, 2011. ISBN: 9780307887436. **SPEC, HUM**

Welcome to the year 2044, a grandly dystopian future where kids like Wade live a largely virtual existence thanks to global warming. Wade lives in a kind of ghetto area called the Stacks, for the stacks of trailers piled everywhere. No wonder he spends most of his time tied into OASIS, "a globally networked virtual reality" that offers players an opportunity to escape the quotidian awfulness of life. Things get complicated when Wade inadvertently happens on a cleverly concealed clue that might be his ticket to wealth and power. But there's no privacy in an online world, and soon Wade and a clutch of his gamer friends find themselves running for their lives from others who want the clue. This is a first novel for Cline, a screenwriter whose 2009 film *Fanboys* has become something of a cult classic. Its obsession with the Star Wars films recalls the numerous (significant) pop culture references in *Ready Player One*.

RED MARS / GREEN MARS / BLUE MARS

Robinson, Kim Stanley. Bantam/Spectra, 1993. ISBN: 0553092049 /
Bantam/Spectra, 1994. ISBN: 0553096400 / Bantam/Spectra, 1996.
ISBN: 0553101447. **SPEC, ALEX**

The red planet gets a full-dress treatment in this ambitious trilogy by a winner of the Hugo, Nebula, Locus, and World Fantasy Awards. Beginning in 2026, the trilogy charts the course of the human colonization of Mars, the shaping of the its ecology and its ultimate terraforming. The social, political, and ecological issues that crop up are not dissimilar to those being discussed, debated, and sometimes derided today as they regard global warming and its ramifications. *Red Mars* tells the story of the establishment of the first settlement on Mars, while *Green Mars* explores the first efforts at terraforming. As the title of the third volume suggests, oceans have now been established. Regard this 1,700-page trilogy as the equivalent of a multivolume world (i.e., Mars) history and you have some idea of its ambition and scope. Happily it is vastly more readable than a textbook. Indeed, many regard it as the premier work of science fiction of the 1990s. Robinson's *Antarctica*, a stand-alone novel, is often compared with the trilogy because its setting, Antarctica, approximates the inhospitable environment of Mars. This novel, however, is as much mystery as science fiction, since it involves the exploitation of the natural resources of Antarctica by multinational corporations and the attempts by "ecoteurs" (think *saboteurs*) to stave this off. Who are the ecoteurs, and will they succeed? Read this brilliantly relevant novel to find out.

THE REHEARSAL

Catton, Eleanor. Little, Brown, 2010. ISBN: 9780316074339. **GF**

This unconventional novel is the story of two neighboring schools: one a private school for girls, the second a school for drama students. The alleged sexual abuse of one of the girls by her adult male music coach provides a focus for the action while also becoming the invasive—and callous—inspiration for a play that the drama students then contrive as the core of their traditional year-end performance. The play rehearsals and the rehearsals of a group of girls for a saxophone recital give the novel its title and provide an opportunity for the author to link performance and real life as the students are also "rehearsing" for their adult lives. The stories of the girls are linked by their teacher, a strong-willed woman who will evoke memories of Muriel Spark's Miss Jean Brodie as she revels in stage-managing her students' lives. As the lines between performance and real life begin to blur, *The Rehearsal* becomes an increasingly challenging novel; contributing to this is the fact that many of the scenes are presented nonchronologically and as if they were scenes in a play, not in a novel. A bit of a tour de force, this first novel was written as the New Zealand author's creative writing master's thesis and was subsequently shortlisted for the *Guardian* First Book Award. Despite—or because of—its complexities, the novel would provide an excellent text for high school drama classes.

RESERVATION BLUES

Alexie, Sherman. Atlantic Monthly, 1995. ISBN: 0871135949. **GF, LOI**

Here is the celebrated Native American author's first novel, an exuberant story about a magic guitar, the devil, and blues music. A stranger, fleeing from the devil—whom he calls "the Gentleman"—arrives one day on the Spokane Indian Reservation, desperate to lose the enchanted guitar the devil, er, Gentleman has given him in exchange for his soul. Young Thomas-Builds-the-Fire gladly—but perhaps unwisely—accepts the instrument, and in short order has formed his own R&B band, along with his friends Victor and Junior. Calling themselves Coyote Springs, the three begin playing in local venues and soon begin touring. The promise of success attracts some wonderfully named groupies—two white girls who are called (à la the Archie comics) Betty and Veronica—and two Native Americans named Chess and Checkers Warm Water. Success is famously problematic, but in this case it's exacerbated by a lingering question: will too much of it attract the Gentleman's attention to them? Alexie brings his wonderfully humorous attitude to material that—though sometimes fantastic—nevertheless paints a realistic and insightful picture of contemporary Native life. His first book for YAs, *The Absolutely True Diary of a Part-Time Indian*, is also not to be missed.

THE RULE OF FOUR

Caldwell, Ian, and Dustin Thomason. Dial, 2004. ISBN: 0385337116. **M/S**

Set at Princeton University, this intellectual mystery puts Dan Brown's *Da Vinci Code* in the shade with its cleverly conceived plot and its fine writing.

Tom and Paul are trying to finish their graduate research on a celebrated but baffling Renaissance manuscript called "Hypnerotomachia Poliphili." They appear to have hit a dead end until a mysterious diary appears and a fellow researcher is murdered! Let the thrills begin as our students rush through a tangle of puzzles, codes, ciphers, and more in an urgent attempt to resolve the manuscript's mysteries before they, too, might become the victims of the murderer. The authors, both Ivy League graduates, certainly know their setting, the social lives and the mindsets of students there. They also know their history and have based their cunning puzzle mystery on an authentic manuscript that is said to contain coded clues to a buried Roman treasure. Quick! Where's my shovel?

RULE OF THE BONE

Banks, Russell. HarperCollins, 1995. ISBN: 0060172754. **GF**

Fourteen-year-old Chappie, a self-described mall rat, lives with his mother and abusive stepfather in upstate New York, where he slips into a disaffected life of drugs and petty theft. Finding himself in trouble with the law, he decides to reinvent himself, getting a crossed bones tattoo on his arm and renaming himself Bone. Perhaps inevitably he then leaves home and takes to the road, living a life of squalor with dopers and a gang of biker thieves. Along the way he rescues a little girl named Rose from a pedophile and then meets a Rastafarian named I-Man, who will lead him on an odyssey of self-discovery that will take him all the way to Jamaica. This is an astonishing novel by one of America's most important writers. Banks has not only demonstrated a great social consciousness in this unforgettable novel but has created an absolutely marvelous character in Chappie/Bone, giving him a pitch-perfect voice with which to tell his story. Published in 1995, this is one of the first contemporary adult crossover novels and remains one of the finest, the kind of book—like *The Catcher in the Rye*—that speaks to and for an entire generation.

SAG HARBOR

Whitehead, Colson. Doubleday, 2009. ISBN: 9780385527651. **GF, LOI**

Set in 1985, author Whitehead's autobiographical novel tells the coming-of-age story of 15-year-old Benji Cooper and his younger brother, Reggie, well-to-do sons of a doctor and a lawyer. Benji (who now prefers to be called Ben) is one of the few black students at his exclusive prep school in New York, where he has the reputation of being a bit of a nerd (who reads *Fangoria* magazine). But the summer months are different. This is when the boys come, every year, to a black enclave in Sag Harbor, "the definition of paradox, black boys with beach houses." Episodic in form, the novel's eight chapters focus, with wit and warmth, on classic adolescent situations from a job scooping ice cream to dreams of dating, from BB guns to beer to nude beaches and, above all else, trying to fit in. This endearing exercise in nostalgia may remind some readers of Ray Bradbury's classic coming-of-age story *Dandelion Wine*.

SAMMY AND JULIANA IN HOLLYWOOD

Sáenz, Benjamin Alire. Cinco Puntos, 2004. ISBN: 0938317814. **GF, LOI**

No, not Hollywood, California, but instead the Hollywood barrio of Las Cruces, New Mexico. Set in the late 1960s, this episodic story recounts the coming-of-age of young Sammy Santos, whose life seems defined by loss, most poignantly that of his mother and of his first love, Juliana. Death is not the only agent of loss, however; sometimes it's society, as is the case with a friend who is drafted for military service in Vietnam and two gay friends of Sammy's who leave the small-town prejudice and homophobia of the barrio for a new life elsewhere. Meanwhile the hard-working Sammy continues to dream of college. An avid reader, he is known at school as "the Librarian" (not a bad thing to be called!). Sáenz, a former priest who now teaches in the MFA program at the University of Texas–El Paso, has a large heart and shows extraordinary empathy for his characters. Many observers regard this book as having been published for teens, as it was shortlisted for the *Los Angeles Times* Book Prize as a teen book. However, since Cinco Puntos has no YA imprint, I think it's fair to include it here.

THE SECRET LIFE OF BEES

Kidd, Sue Monk. Viking, 2002. ISBN: 0670894605. **HIST, LOI**

Kidd's story of life in South Carolina in 1964 has become a mini-classic of adult fiction for young adults. Following the accidental death of her mother, Lily Owens—now 14—has been raised by her family's strong-minded African American housekeeper, Rosaleen. Fleeing from their rural home in Sylvan following a violent racial incident that left Rosaleen injured, the two find themselves in the small town of Tiburon, where they meet three beekeeping African American sisters: August, June, and May Boatwright. The three provide refuge and new lives for Lily and Rosaleen. Lily learns about beekeeping, honey, and the Black Madonna venerated by the Boatwrights. In the process she finds her first real home and discovers secrets about her late mother and her connection to Tiburon. Beautifully and evocatively written, *The Secret Life of Bees* is a paean to the powers of sisterhood, truth, and love.

SHADES OF GREY: THE ROAD TO HIGH SAFFRON
Fforde, Jasper. Viking, 2009. ISBN: 9780670019632. **SPEC, HUM**

That darned future! Something's always going wrong there. This time it's a mysterious something called, er, "Something Happened," and it's left the world at the mercy of a Colortocracy. Come again? Well, it simply means the world—and one's place in it—are dictated by the color individuals see. Thus, those who see only grey are virtual outcasts. Eddie Russett, our hero in this first volume of a promised series, can see red, which means he's fairly well placed and will move even further up the ladder when he marries Constance Oxblood. But then he falls in love with a young woman who is, wouldn't you just know it, a grey. And then things get really interesting with the advent of carnivorous trees, an UnLibrary, terrible secrets, and more. So much more that one quickly sees why Fforde has been called both a modern Kafka and also a modern C. S. Lewis (some combination, no?).

Fforde made his debut with another triumph of imagination titled *The Eyre Affair*, starring a character named Thursday Next who lives in an alternative England where she works in the Literary Detective Division of the Special Operations Network. Time travel features in this one, along with pet dodos and the kidnapping of characters escaped from famous novels—novels such as . . . *Jane Eyre*. Clearly it's easier to read Fforde's brilliantly imagined novels than it is to describe them, so get busy reading!

SKIPPY DIES
Murray, Paul. Faber and Faber, 2010. ISBN: 9780865479432. **GF**

No spoiler here. The titular character, Skippy, a 14-year-old student at Seabrook College, a historic Catholic boy's school in Dublin, is, indeed, a goner by page

5 of the prologue. His last words are "Tell Lori I love her." What follows this dramatic declaration is an extended flashback explaining the circumstances of Skippy's life leading up to his death. It turns out that Skippy was not the only one in love with the irresistible Lori—so was his bête noire, the psychopathic, drug-dealing fellow student Carl. Also in love, though not with Lori, is history teacher Howard (the coward) Fallon, whose heart belongs to the attractive substitute teacher Miss McIntyre. Far more than a love story, this is a darkly unconventional but often hilarious study of adolescence that also charts the lives of Skippy's best friends Ruprecht, who is devoted to string theory; Mario, who is devoted to girls; and Dennis, who is devoted to, well, cynicism. A classic school story like *Skippy Dies* needs to explore not only the heart but also the mind, and this doesn't disappoint, examining the intersections of science, metaphysics, and the interconnectedness of past and present. Extravagant, challenging, and compelling, this is a novel not to be missed.

SNOW FALLING ON CEDARS

Guterson, David. Harcourt, 1994. ISBN: 0151001006. **HIST, M/S, LOI**

Guterson's first novel is set in 1954 in the Puget Sound area, where a local fisherman is found drowned under mysterious circumstances. In the ensuing investigation another fisherman, Japanese American Kabuo Miyamoto, is charged with the crime, and the novel then becomes a courtroom drama compelling enough to rival John Grisham's set pieces. Complicating the plot is the fact that local newspaperman Ishmael Chambers finds evidence that could alter the course of the trial. However, the fact that the woman he once loved married Miyamoto instead means he must wrestle with a moral choice. The novel is further enriched by its evocation of another issue of morality: the internment of local Japanese Americans during World War II. Another novel that also deals with this still resonant issue is Julie Otsuka's *When the Emperor Was Divine*.

SNOW IN AUGUST

Hamill, Pete. Little, Brown, 1997. ISBN: 0316340944. **HIST, ALEX**

Michael Devlin, a preadolescent Irish Catholic, lives with his widowed mother in a Brooklyn tenement in the late 1940s. On his way to mass one evening where he serves as an altar boy, Michael happens to meet an immigrant Orthodox rabbi named Hirsh, and an improbable friendship begins. Michael teaches the rabbi English and baseball, while the rabbi teaches Michael Yiddish and tells him fabulous stories rooted in Jewish history and folklore (think Isaac Bashevis Singer). Unfortunately a neighborhood gang, consumed by anti-Semitism, learn of Michael's friendship and beat him up, then assault his mother and finally beat Rabbi Hirsh nearly to death. Determined that this shall never happen again, Michael calls on the Jewish traditions he has learned with surprising and satisfying results. No one knows working-class New York life better than journalist Hamill, who has been a columnist and editor for both the *New York Post* and the *New York Daily News*. *Snow in August* is a superbly realized book with two wonderful characters who will resonate with adult and young adult readers alike. Readers who want to know more about Hamill might wish to read his memoir, *A Drinking Life*.

SPECIAL TOPICS IN CALAMITY PHYSICS

Pessl, Marisha. Viking, 2006. ISBN: 067003777X. **M/S**

Blue van Meer's life has been a peripatetic one, thanks to her father's penchant for serving as a visiting lecturer at one obscure small college after another. Now that she's a high school senior, however, she and her single-parent father seem to have settled down, and she's enrolled in the exclusive St. Gallway School in Stockton, North Carolina. To her considerable surprise she finds herself a popular kid, one of a charmed circle called the Bluebloods, and the protégé of the mysterious film studies teacher Hannah Schneider. When a friend of Hannah's is murdered at a party the Bluebloods have crashed, the novel takes on the air of a Hitchcock movie—a natural for a film buff like Blue. Pessl's first novel is often arch and self-conscious in a postmodern way and filled with cinematic and literary allusions. Structured as a syllabus for a Great Works of Literature class, the novel is intended to evoke the style if not the spirit of the late Russian American novelist Vladimir Nabokov. Not as sophisticated as Nabokov and not as academic as this sounds, the novel is both accessible and intriguing. It was selected by the *New York Times* as one of the best books of the year. Readers of this will also enjoy Gregory Galloway's *As Simple as Snow*.

STAR ISLAND

Hiaasen, Carl. Knopf, 2010. ISBN: 9780307272584. **M/S, HUM**

Now that the great Donald E. Westlake has passed away, Carl Hiaasen is inarguably the funniest mystery novelist still writing. Any one of his hilarious novels could have been chosen for this collection, but *Star Island* seems especially appropriate since it is both recent and also features a 20-something protagonist named Ann DeLusia who is a double for legendarily dissolute pop star Cherry Pye. Whenever Pye's antics have rendered her unable to appear, Ann is called into service. Things lurch along like this with a reasonable degree of success and secrecy until Ann is kidnapped by a hapless paparazzi and the wheels threaten to come off the bus. The consequences are complicated and genuinely funny. Readers of the author's previous books will be delighted by the reappearance of the character named Skink, a former governor of Florida who has taken to the swamps, where he lives off the land—and assorted roadkill. Skink is particularly cranky about unscrupulous developers who are destroying the Florida ecosystem, and once again he finds one of those involved in this plot. Can chastisement be far behind? Nope! One could say more, but why spoil the fun of discovery? A columnist for the *Miami Herald*, Hiaasen is also the author of three books for children, one of which—*Hoot*—was selected as a Newbery Honor title.

STARDUST

Gaiman, Neil. Avon/Spike, 1999. ISBN: 0380977281. **SPEC, ALEX**

Thanks in part to the enormous success of his Sandman graphic novels, British author Gaiman is now almost in the same lofty league as Stephen King when it comes to popularity with YAs. Though typically more benign than King, Gaiman too fills his work with fantastic creatures and otherworldly premises and settings. Case in point: *Stardust*—arguably his most popular work with YAs—which is set in the realm of Faerie. To it one fine day goes 17-year-old Tristran Thorn in search of a falling star that he has promised to his girlfriend. That Tristran is only half human (!) and that the star is not a star and that he is far from the only one after the st—er, whatever it is— will only add to the complications that ensue (many of them quite funny). This was turned into a not terribly successful 2007 movie starring the likes of Claire Danes, Michelle Pfeiffer, Robert De Niro, and Charlie Cox.

Gaiman fans will also want to investigate his later novel *Anansi Boys*. As delightful as *Stardust*, this has as its conceit that our protagonists, brothers named Fat Charlie Nancy and Spider, are both the sons of the trickster god Anansi from whom they have inherited certain special . . . abilities. Spider has a penchant for using these to make Charlie's life miserable and readers' lives quite happy.

THE STORY OF EDGAR SAWTELLE

Wroblewski, David. Ecco, 2008. ISBN: 9780061374227. **GF**

A remarkable first novel by a 48-year-old software developer, this story of Edgar Sawtelle, a mute boy growing up in rural Wisconsin with his dog-breeding parents, has garnered both critical and popular raves. Edgar has been born mute, but his incapacity to speak is no problem with the dogs, which Edgar helps train. He is especially close to Almondine, a dog of rare breed who manages a special communication with him. It's a good life until the boy's Uncle Claude returns to the farm. The boy's father then dies under suspicious circumstances—could Uncle Claude be complicit?—and Edgar, who wonders just that, is forced to flee into the woods accompanied only by three puppies. The novel's unusual point of view, obvious gloss on *Hamlet*, and sympathetic characters make this a natural read for YAs, despite the book's considerable heft (562 pages). Another recommended novel that finds inspiration in *Hamlet* is Matt Haig's *The Dead Fathers Club*.

SUMMER BLONDE

Tomine, Adrian. Drawn and Quarterly, 2002. ISBN: 1896597491. **GN, GF, LOI**

Graphic artist Tomine, who began publishing when he was 16 and is now in his 20s, sprang to prominence with his series of comics called Optic Nerve. *Summer Blonde* is a collection of four of those stories that evoke the work of Raymond Carver. Okay, to be fair, this is a claim of his publisher, but nevertheless, the statement is certainly true in terms of Tomine's moody, often noirish atmosphere. As for content, the work is more akin to Daniel Clowes. For example, one of the stories here is about a shy novelist with writer's block (Tomine himself?) who goes in search of the girl he was obsessed with in high school; in a second story, two high school outcasts are brought together in the gloomy shadow of the first Gulf War. Tomine fans may also want to have a look at a more recent, highly praised example of his work, *Shortcomings*, a full-length novel about the life and relationships of a San Francisco movie theater manager named Ben Tanaka (who, in his solipsism and general unpleasantness, is a bit of an antihero).

SUNDAY YOU LEARN HOW TO BOX

Wright, Bil. Scribner, 2000. ISBN: 0684857952. **GF, LOI**

Set in a Connecticut housing project in 1968, this first novel is the story of 14-year-old Louis Bowman, who is beginning to recognize his homosexuality. To spare him assaults from the neighborhood boys, his alcohol-abusing, misguided mother forces him to take Sunday boxing lessons from his stepfather, Ben, who welcomes the opportunity to knock Louis around. At the same time, the boy is developing a major crush on the neighborhood "hoodlum," Ray Anthony Robinson. The enigmatic Ray gradually accepts Louis's friendship and becomes his unofficial protector. This fine novel was an Alex Award book and also a New York Public Library Best Book for the Teen Age.

SWAMPLANDIA!

Russell, Karen. Knopf, 2011. ISBN: 9780307263995. **GF**

The eponymous Swamplandia!, an Everglades-based alligator-wrestling theme park, is in decline thanks to the recent death of its star performer and sudden competition for tourist dollars from World of Darkness, the newly opened rival park. The family that operates Swamplandia!, the self-styled Bigtree clan, is also in gradual dissolution. Our narrator, 13-year-old Ava, tells of her brother Kiwi's defection to the rival park, her sister Ossie's elopement with a (maybe) ghost, and her father Chief Bigtree's disappearance. This leaves Ava to manage the park and, more important, to save her family, even if it means traveling to the very gates of hell. If this sounds like a fantasy, it's not—quite. But it is an example of American magical realism, wrought with wonderful imagination and wit. If a measure of a book's originality is the difficulty it poses to a reviewer who tries to synopsize it, this is one of the most original novels of the last twenty years! And, indeed, so it is. To find such a sui generis work of fiction is cause for celebration. Russell's first book, the wonderfully titled short story collection *St. Lucy's Home for Girls Raised by Wolves*, was equally lauded by critics, and one of the stories in the collection inspired *Swamplandia!*

10TH GRADE
Weisberg, Joseph. Random House, 2002. ISBN: 0375505849. **GF, ALEX**

Weisberg's first novel is the coming-of-age story of New Jersey tenth grader Jeremy Reskin. Told in his first person, ungrammatical voice that is authentically his own, the story—presented as Jeremy's journal—charts his sophomore year in high school, much of which is devoted to appreciating (i.e., ogling) the female form divine, especially that of his Spanish conversation partner and would-be love of his life, Renee Shopmaker. In the meantime Jeremy is also engaged in a sort-of relationship with another girl, Gillian. Then there's his soccer playing, his family—lawyer dad, housewife mom, and two (ugh) sisters—and, finally, there's the prom, where Jeremy enjoys a sexual initiation of sorts and, in its wake, considers establishing a real relationship with the pulchritudinous Renee. Will he? It seems the reader—and Jeremy—will have to await his junior year to find that out.

THE THINGS THEY CARRIED
O'Brien, Tim. Houghton Mifflin, 1990. ISBN: 039551598X. **HIST**

With his first novel, the National Book Award–winning *Going After Cacciato*, O'Brien became a kind of poet laureate of the Vietnam War. He cemented this reputation with his second book, this brilliant collection of twenty-two short stories about a platoon of young American soldiers in Vietnam. Though the stories are individual—and many are based on O'Brien's own experiences—they cohere beautifully to form a novel in the form of stories. Published nearly a quarter of a century ago, the stories remain as fresh and immediate as they were when first published. It's hard to believe that today's teens would regard this as historical fiction, but when one considers that it was their grandfathers who might have fought in this war, it is inarguably the case. The enduing value of this book is nevertheless evidenced by the fact that the *New York Times* named it to its Books of the Century List, saying, "It belongs high on the list of best fiction about any war." And so it does.

THE THIRD ANGEL

Hoffman, Alice. Crown, 2008. ISBN: 9780307393852. **ROM, SPEC**

There are three angels, one of Hoffman's characters claims: the angel of life, the angel of death, and a third angel, "the one who walks among us." The highly successful author of more than two dozen works of fiction puts the equation to the test in this collection of three interrelated short stories set over a period of years. Aside from their thematic unity, what connects the stories is their physical setting: a haunted London hotel that adds a ghostly quality to these three tales of star-crossed love and the search for faith.

A great favorite of teen girl readers, Hoffman writes both adult books (like this one) and titles published as YA. In terms of reader appeal it's hard to go wrong with either category. Hoffman devotees will doubtless also want to read her novel *Here on Earth*. Its protagonist, March, should never have returned to her hometown with only her teenage daughter for company (or chaperonage [*sic*]), since an encounter with an old flame rekindles a forbidden romance. What more does one need to say?

THE TIME TRAVELER'S WIFE

Niffenegger, Audrey. MacAdam Cage, 2003. ISBN: 193156146X. **ROM, SPEC, ALEX**

A love story with a twist: one of the partners suffers from something called chrono-displacement, which means, in layman's language, that he is a time traveler. Worse, he has no control over when his journeys will happen or what he might be doing at the time. Thus, when the traveler, Henry DeTamble—36 at the time—first appears to the woman who will become his wife, she is 6, and he appears out of nowhere, stark naked (don't worry—nothing untoward happens). Time travel is tricky and sometimes head-scratchingly complex, as when Henry encounters himself in his travels or when he and Clare ultimately marry and she is 23 and he is 31, five years younger than when they first met. Happily, the novel is told from both partners' points of view, which helps keep the story on the rails. They say that absence makes the heart grow fonder, and Henry's frequent disappearances seem only to strengthen his and Clare's marriage, which suggests that Niffenegger's first novel is more interested in romance than in science fiction. It's worth noting, by the way, that Henry is a librarian working at Chicago's Newberry Library, though this will be of greater interest to similar working professionals than to most teens.

The author's second novel, *Her Fearful Symmetry*, is another genre-blender, this one a romance and ghost story that features mirror-image (female) twins, a London apartment bordering a cemetery, a despondent lover, and a crossword-puzzle crafter who suffers from obsessive-compulsive disorder. Be still my heart . . .

TO SAY NOTHING OF THE DOG; OR, HOW WE FOUND THE BISHOP'S BIRD STUMP AT LAST

Willis, Connie. Bantam/Spectra, 1998. ISBN: 0553099957. **SPEC, HUM, ALEX**

Winner of multiple Hugo and Nebula Awards (six apiece!), Willis is no slouch at writing science fiction, as she proves in spades in this delightfully wacky time travel fiction. The year is 2057, and the wealthy and redoubtable Lady Shrapnell (no foolin') has offered to fund the Oxford University time travel project in exchange for help in restoring Coventry Cathedral, destroyed by the Nazis in 1940. This means considerable time travel, and poor, time-lagged Ned Henry must return to the year 1888 in search of a monstrosity called— you guessed it—the Bishop's Bird Stump. The fly in the stump, er, *ointment* is that Ned must also correct an anomaly that might alter the future in such a way that Germany will win World War II. Yikes! Meanwhile the invocations of classic British popular fiction ranging from Jerome K. Jerome's *Three Men in a Boat* to Dorothy L. Sayers's mysteries may remind some readers of Jasper Fforde's *The Eyre Affair*. This thoroughly delightful romp was—not surprisingly—selected as an Alex Award winner.

THE TRUE ACCOUNT

Mosher, Howard Frank. Houghton Mifflin, 2003. ISBN: 0618197214. **HIST, HUM**

This marvelous and hilarious picaresque recounts the improbable journey west of young Ticonderoga and his eccentric, madcap uncle, the would-be inventor and teacher True Teague Kinneson. Their goal is to beat Lewis and Clark to the Pacific. Needless to say their journey is a good deal more adventurous (misadventurous?) than the official expedition. Though Ticonderoga is our narrator, speaking in a delightfully vernacular nineteenth-century voice, it is his uncle who is the main attraction, a walking grab bag of eccentricities and a copper dome that protects his head—injured, he claims, when he was with Ethan Allen at Fort Ticonderoga. Some more dubious readers may suspect that alcohol was involved. Readers who enjoy this—and who wouldn't—may want to look for two similar-in-spirit earlier novels, Robert Lewis Taylor's Pulitzer Prize winner *The Travels of Jamie McPheeters* and Thomas Berger's *Little Big Man*.

2030: THE REAL STORY OF WHAT HAPPENS TO AMERICA

Brooks, Albert. St. Martin's Press, 2011. ISBN: 9780312583729. **GF, HUM, SPEC**

This first novel by humorist, screenwriter, director, and comic actor Brooks is not exactly a laugh riot but something better: a thought-provoking near dystopian novel of singular relevance to young adults. The premise is that by 2030 cancer has been cured! As a result, older Americans are living longer—much longer. And as a result they are commanding the lion's share of the country's resources for which the younger generation has to pay, leaving it with less—much less. Accordingly, young Americans are beginning to resent older Americans, and the resentment is starting to manifest itself in violence. Indeed, one of the young characters has formed a terrorist cell. But before much can happen in this regard, something else happens: the big one hits Los Angeles, a 9.1 earthquake followed by two 8-plus aftershocks. The city, unsurprisingly, is destroyed. But it will cost trillions of dollars to rebuild, and the federal government simply doesn't have the money. Where will it come from? Can you say "China," boys and girls? At this point the novel moves from dystopian to cautionary, but in both cases the most affected Americans are the younger ones, some no more than young adults. Hence, the urgent relevance of this compelling novel. To say that every YA should read it makes it sound didactic, and it's not, not at all. It's funny where it needs to be, suspenseful where it needs to be, and cautionary where it—well, you get the idea. Yes, it's highly recommended.

UNSEEN ACADEMICALS

Pratchett, Terry. HarperCollins, 2009. ISBN: 9780061161704. **SPEC**

British fantasist Pratchett was recently named recipient of YALSA's prestigious Edwards Award for the body of his work. Here in this recent Discworld novel he demonstrates why. A bit reminiscent of a Harry You-Know-Who tale, this tells the story of how the wizards of Unseen University find themselves need-ing to win a football game—without resorting to magic. Fortunately they are coached by Mr. Nutt, a candle dipper who is also a goblin. Or is he? A gob-lin, that is. There's no question about his candle dipping . . . Pratchett was knighted the same year this novel was published for his "services to litera-ture." Thus, he is now Sir Terry! And don't you forget it. It should be noted, at least in passing, that Sir Terry also writes for young adults, and in fact, his wonderful, deeply felt novel *Nation*, written for teenagers, was a Printz Award winner.

UPSTATE

Buckhanon, Kalisha. St. Martin's Press, 2005. ISBN: 0312332688. **GF, LOI, ALEX**

This moving epistolary novel tells the story—in letters they exchange—of star-crossed lovers Antonio and Natasha. The lives of the two Harlem teens are turned upside down when Antonio is convicted of murdering his father and is sent upstate to jail. Beginning in the 1990s, the letters continue for ten years as the two grow up and mature. In the process their lives inevitably change as do their feelings for each other. Natasha, proving to be an excellent student, pursues higher education and finally becomes an attorney; meanwhile a rev-elation about Antonio will also change his life dramatically. But will the two young people be able to revive their relationship? Buckhanon's second novel, *Conception*, is somewhat less successful but still well worth reading. It's the unusual story of a 15-year-old African American girl who is pregnant by a married man. She dreams of aborting her baby, but (here's the unusual part) the unborn baby also dreams—of the three previous times it has failed to be born. Will this finally be the one in which it finds life?

THE VANISHING OF KATHARINA LINDEN

Grant, Helen. Delacorte, 2010. ISBN: 9780385344173. **M/S**

When Pia's grandmother dies in a freak accident, the 10-year-old finds her-self a local outcast in the small German town of Bad Müenstereifel. Her only friend is Stink Stefan, the most unpopular boy in school. When these two subsequently decide to investigate a town mystery—the disappearance of local girls—they find inspiration in the ghost stories that an elderly neighbor,

Herr Schiller, tells them. Though the two youngsters naively suspect that the girls have been spirited away by supernatural forces, the truth is closer to reality—and far more dangerous. Grant's first novel, a blend of suspense and horror, tells a compellingly readable story with a richly realized setting, a small town where everyday life is never far from a haunted past.

Grant's second novel, *The Glass Demon*, is equally teen-friendly and, like the first, is set in Germany. It too involves deaths and more than a whiff of the supernatural, this time involving something called Bonschariant, a demon that haunts glass. It's enough to make you throw away your mirrors!

WATER FOR ELEPHANTS
Gruen, Sara. Algonquin, 2006. ISBN: 1565124995. **ROM, HIST, ALEX**

Told by nonagenarian Jacob Jankowski, this novel of reminiscence is set during the Great Depression of the 1930s when Jacob, a young almost-veterinarian (he has been forced by the accidental death of his parents to abandon his studies less than a year shy of his degree), joins the circus, specifically the Benzini Brothers Most Spectacular Show on Earth. There he is charged with caring for the menagerie of the shabby traveling circus, which includes an elephant named Rosie that Jacob comes to love. He also falls in love with the circus's equestrienne, a beautiful young woman named Marlena. Unfortunately she is married to the circus boss, the sometimes sadistic August, who has been known to mercilessly beat Rosie and also Marlena when he is in his cups (which is often). While the romance will capture the reader's attention, it is the careful reconstruction and evocation of circus life in the '30s that is the novel's most distinguishing and memorable feature.

WHAT GIRLS LEARN
Cook, Karin. Pantheon, 1997. ISBN: 0679448284. **GF, ALEX**

Published in 1997 and named an Alex Award winner for 1999, Cook's first novel is the poignant story of two sisters, Tilden (the narrator) and Elizabeth. Their romantic mother Frances, a divorcée, moves with her daughters from their home in Atlanta to New York, where she meets Nick, falls in love, and marries him. The girls, naturally, feel uprooted. The relationship between the two sisters becomes edgier as Elizabeth, the younger and more vivacious sister, fits into her new environment quickly while Tilden remains an outsider. As Tilden turns 13 and Elizabeth 12, sex becomes a disconcerting issue for them. But there's worse to come: Frances discovers a lump in her breast, and life becomes more than an exercise in fitting in—it becomes a study in survival. This is a quintessential crossover novel that could have easily been published as YA, though adults have certainly found as much to like here as teens. Cook, a graduate of Vassar College and New York University's Creative Writing Program, currently works as the development officer of the Door, a multiservice youth center.

WHAT I WAS

Rosoff, Meg. Viking, 2008. ISBN: 9780670018444. **HIST, LOI**

The first two novels of author Rosoff, an American living in England, were published for teenagers rather than for adults. Indeed, one of them, *How I Live Now*, won the Printz Award. But this novel, her third, was published in England first, then brought over here and published as an adult book. Why? The cynical answer would be that someone at Rosoff's publishing house decided the book would be more profitable if it were published on the adult side. The more charitable answer is that the frame story—a 100-year-old man's reminiscences—along with the novel's sedate pace and fairly cerebral tone would not attract young adult readers. I would argue that despite the narrator's age, the novel will be of interest to YAs, since its focus is the man's boarding school years, when he meets another boy named Finn while running on the beach. He and Finn, a solitary boy living in a rude hut on the shore, become best friends and perhaps more. Readers of this luminous fiction will decide for themselves.

WHEN THE EMPEROR WAS DIVINE

Otsuka, Julie. Knopf, 2002. ISBN: 0375414290. **HIST, LOI, ALEX**

Set during World War II, this universally praised first novel tells the sad story of a Japanese American family who—following the arrest of the father for alleged conspiracy—are taken from their Berkeley, California, home to an internment camp, where they are forced to spend the next three years in deplorable conditions. The story continues when the family returns to Berke-

ley to find their home trashed by vandals and a climate of continuing prejudice and racial hatred there. Otsuka tells the story from the shifting points of
view of each member of the family—mother, 11-year-old daughter, 8-year-old
son, and father—in quiet, understated prose that is made only more powerful
by its subtlety. Though small in size, the book contains large truths that young
adults need to know. Readers of this novel will also want to read Guterson's
Snow Falling on Cedars.

WHEN WE GET THERE

Seliy, Shauna. Bloomsbury, 2007. ISBN: 9781596913509. **GF, LOI**

Thirteen-year-old Lucas's mother has vanished in the wake of the death of her
coal miner husband in an underground explosion. She has left the boy in the
care of his grandmother, Slats, with the stern admonition that he is not to go
in search of her. Of course, he immediately does and quickly learns that he is
not the only one who is searching: a possibly deranged local man, Zoli, is also
looking. What to make of this? And what has happened to Lucas's mother?
And will the boy realize his late father's dream of finding, in the Allegheny
Forest, a place called Heart's Content? There will be answers to these questions and the search for them is certainly compelling, but what really distinguishes this first novel is its beautifully realized setting—the western Pennsyl-
vania coal country—and Lucas's huge extended family of Russian, Croatian,
and Hungarian extraction. In my starred *Booklist* review of this novel I wrote,
"The word 'lovely' might well have been coined for the express purpose of
describing the sensibility that informs this splendid first novel." That was
written in 2007, and it remains as true today as it was then. An unforgettable,
heart-touching novel.

WHEN WE WERE ROMANS

Kneale, Matthew. Doubleday/Talese, 2008. ISBN: 9780385526258. **GF**

Told in the voice of 9-year-old Lawrence (complete with misspellings and
grammatical and syntactical quirks), this is the haunting story of how the
boy's mother takes him and his younger sister, Jemima, on a trip to Rome,
where she had lived years before and where she hopes old friends will give
them a temporary home. The catalyst for this hasty and ill-planned trip is

the mother's paranoid fear that her ex-husband will harm her and her family. Lawrence knows that sometimes his mum gets "stuck," as he puts it, and it's up to him to give her a little push to bring her back to normal. Sadly, "normal" becomes less and less a part of their lives. Though Lawrence doesn't realize it, older readers will understand his mother is mentally ill (she's probably a paranoid schizophrenic). Kneale, a winner of England's prestigious Whitbread Prize for his previous novel *English Passengers* (which was also short-listed for the Booker Prize), once again demonstrates his singular skills in this new novel as he invests Lawrence's innocent perspective with symbolic underpinnings in the form of the boy's fascination with the insane Roman emperors Nero and Caligula. This is a sad but brilliantly conceived and written novel that deserves a wide readership.

WICKED

Maguire, Gregory. HarperCollins, 1995. ISBN: 0060391448. **SPEC**

Maguire's wickedly clever reimagining of *The Wizard of Oz* has become virtually a household name thanks to the enormous success of the Broadway musical that is based upon it. With or without the musical accompaniment, however, *Wicked* the novel stands tall and proud on its own merits. In Maguire's revisionist version of the classic Baum tale, it is not Dorothy Gale of Kansas who is the protagonist but, rather, the Wicked Witch of the West, whom the author dubs Elphaba. Born with emerald green skin and unusual teeth, Elphaba grows up an outsider, goes off to college—where she rooms with a dippy socialite named Glinda—and ultimately becomes an animal rights activist in a Land of Oz that is ruled by a dictator Wizard who has made the kingdom more dystopia than fairyland. As if that's not enough, Dorothy doesn't enter the picture until very near the end of the book. Take that, Baum purists! Maguire has subsequently written three other volumes to complete his Oz cycle: *Son of a Witch, A Lion among Men,* and *Out of Oz.*

WINTER'S BONE

Woodrell, Daniel. Little, Brown, 2006. ISBN: 031605755X. **GF**

Sixteen-year-old Ree Dolly's good-for-nothing, drug-making (call it "crank cooking") father has jumped bail, and if Ree can't find him and bring him back within a week, she will lose the family house and she, her two younger brothers, and their mentally ill mother will be out on the street. Of course, finding him is easier said than done, since turning to the family for help is not only frustrating but downright dangerous, for these are Ozark Mountain people who don't welcome visitors, not even if they're kin. "Talkin' causes witnesses," they say tersely. Fans of Southern gothic fiction will embrace this wonderful but occasionally bleak novel, which—at its best—evokes the spirit of Flannery O'Connor. There is no higher praise than that! And whether Ree's odyssey will find success is a mystery that will hold readers' rapt attention until the final page.

This novel is a sequel of sorts to Woodrell's earlier novel *Give Us a Kiss: A Country Noir*, which focuses on the Redmonds, a rival drug-dealing family.

WONDER WHEN YOU'LL MISS ME

Davis, Amanda. Morrow, 2003. ISBN: 0688167810. **GF, ALEX**

Faith, 16, is a formerly fat girl who has slimmed down following a brutal attack that inspires a (failed) suicide attempt and sends her to the hospital. The trouble is, the fat girl she was is still alive and well and mouthy inside her, urging her—when she returns to school—to take revenge on those who hurt her. When she finally does, Faith and her internal succubus run away to join the circus. There, surrounded by misfits like herself, Faith pursues a new life and new self. Davis brings an unusual and memorable take to an all-too-familiar problem—teenage cruelty—while also doing a fine job of creating a realistic circus milieu that recalls another circus novel, *Water for Elephants*.

THE YEAR OF ICE

Malloy, Brian. St. Martin's, 2002. ISBN: 0312289480. **GF, LOI, ALEX**

Set in Minneapolis in the 1970s, this is the compelling story of 18-year-old Kevin Doyle, who is attempting to deal with the accidental death of his mother, killed in an automobile accident when her car spun out of control on icy pavement. But it is also the story of Kevin's growing awareness of his homosexuality and his struggle to deal with this. His efforts to remain closeted become more difficult as he attempts to stave off the interest of girls attracted by his good looks and to keep secret his love for his classmate Jon. In the meantime his binge-drinking, irresponsible father, Pat, is also being pursued by women and turns to Kevin for help in resisting *their* advances. These twin efforts by father and son are not without their moments of humor, as is their basic relationship, but things become darker as the boy begins to suspect that his father's philandering may have been the cause of his mother's death. A compelling coming-of-age story, this first novel is an Alex Award winner.

YOUTH IN REVOLT: THE JOURNALS OF NICK TWISP

Payne, C. D. Aivia, 1993. ISBN: 1882647009. **GF, HUM**

Here is yet another cult classic that found a mainstream audience when a movie version was made of it, this one starring Michael Cera. *Youth in Revolt* is actually three novels bound together as one: Book I is "Youth in Revolt," Book II is "Youth in Bondage," and Book III is "Youth in Exile." All are told in the wonderfully idiosyncratic voice of Nick Twisp, who is 14 when we first meet him. Like *Pygmy* (see above) his voice is arguably the most memorable thing about him. Here's a sample of Nickspeak:

> My last name, which I loathe, is Twisp. Even John Wayne on a horse would look effeminate pronouncing that name. As soon as I'm twenty-one, I'm going to jettison it for something a bit more macho. Right now, I'm leaning toward Dillinger. "Nick Dillinger." I think that strikes just the right note of virility.

Speaking of virility, Nick may be, er, revolting, but his idea of revolution has a lot more to do with losing his virginity than overturning the government. The object of his affection is the beauteous—to him, anyway—Sheeni Saunders. The kids live in Oakland, California, and their destinies will involve coming of age, dealing with divorcing parents (Nick's), experiencing the horrors of high school (both), dealing with forty-eight cans of garbanzo beans, and more, much more (the book is five hundred pages long).

Kids will think this is a hoot; many adults will agree, but a word to the wise: the boy does have a mouth on him, and he is, let us not forget, obsessed with S. E. X. Don't say I didn't tell you so.

NONFICTION

ADV = adventure and exploration

ALEX = Alex Award winner

B/M = biography and memoir

GN = graphic novel

GNF = general nonfiction

HIST = historical fiction

HUM = humor

LOI = literature of inclusion

P = poetry

SCI = science and nature

SPO = sports

TECH = technology

AGE OF BRONZE: A THOUSAND SHIPS

Shanower, Eric. Image Comics, 2001. ISBN: 9781582402000. **GN, HIST**

Here is volume 1 of Shanower's ongoing epic graphic novel retelling of the Trojan War. When the author/artist first undertook this project, he estimated it would take nine years to complete. At this writing ten years have passed, and the end is still not in sight. Along the way Shanower has collected two Eisner Awards for his efforts (the Eisners are the Oscars of the graphic novel world) and the allegiance of countless fans. What distinguishes this particular effort—aside from the creative imagination Shanower brings to his retelling of this world classic—is the prodigious research he devotes to ensuring the accuracy of every detail, both textual and visual. The result is an authentic depiction of the classical world that provides the epic's setting. Shanower's art is not only authentic and apposite; it is masterful in its use of black and white and beautiful in its careful draftsmanship. If ever a graphic novel deserved to be called art, it is this brilliant undertaking.

ALL OVER BUT THE SHOUTIN'

Bragg, Rick. Pantheon, 1997. ISBN: 0679442588. **B/M, LOI, ALEX**

A Pulitzer Prize–winning national correspondent for the *New York Times*, journalist Bragg has written a memoir of his early life (he was born in 1959) growing up in near poverty in the American South. He was the second of three sons of an abusive, alcoholic father who died at age 40. Somehow Bragg's mother, whom he clearly adores, provided love and back-breaking hard work, scrimping, saving, and doing without, to keep her family together. Bragg doesn't spare his readers his anger, and some reviewers have found this and his tendency to dwell on his own accomplishments annoying. But teens will identify with the emotional tenor of the book and be gratified by Bragg's ultimate success and the realization of his lifelong dream: to buy his mother a house of her own.

AMERICAN SHAOLIN

Polly, Matthew. Gotham, 2007. ISBN: 9781592402625. **B/M, ALEX**

Polly, a Princeton graduate and Rhodes Scholar, spent two years in China in the early 1990s determined to transform his anemic-looking body into a fighting machine, as it were. His destination was the Shaolin Monastery, birthplace of kung fu and home to a celebrated cadre of fighting monks. The elaborate subtitle of his book speaks volumes about his adventure: *Flying Kicks, Buddhist Monks, and the Legend of the Iron Crotch: An Odyssey in the New China*. In addition to vivid and often droll accounts of his training and various bouts of kung fu action, Polly also gives some serious attention to the changing culture of Communist China in the wake of the Tiananmen Square massacre.

AMERICAN VOYEUR

Denizet-Lewis, Benoit. Simon & Schuster, 2010. ISBN: 9781416539155. **GNF, LOI**

The author, a freelance journalist, delivers sixteen articles that were originally published in such sources as the *New York Times Magazine*, *Spin*, and *Slate*. Deftly combining journalism and sociology, he examines some of the further reaches of modern culture such as life on the "down low," that is, black men living as heterosexuals while secretly engaging in gay sex; and also the desperate lives of homeless gay teens living in San Francisco's Castro District. Denizet-Lewis's interest in youth culture and considerations of sexual identity is manifest in the large number of his essays and reports that feature this age group and topic—pieces like a fascinating look at contemporary teen dating practices, the lives of young gay married men, a middle school transgender girl living as a boy, and more. What lends these pieces their particular immediacy is the author's practice of what he calls "immersion journalism": spending a great deal of time in the company of his subjects to establish emotional rapport or, as he puts it, "waiting around for people to be themselves"—and recognizing and recording those moments when they are.

AND THE PURSUIT OF HAPPINESS

Kalman, Maira. Penguin Press, 2010. ISBN: 9781594202674. **GN, GNF**

Borrowing a celebrated phrase from the Declaration of Independence for her title, gifted artist Kalman offers a wonderfully idiosyncratic celebration in words and pictures of a beautiful America and its democratic form of government. Her strategy is simple: beginning with the January inauguration of Barack Obama, Kalman offers a month-by-month, yearlong journey across America that winds leisurely from coast to coast. Each month on the way is devoted to a separate theme; thus, February offers an affectionate nod to Abraham Lincoln; March reports on "the essence of democracy," a town hall meeting; August features America's immigrant population; and so forth and so on to December's evocation of our first president, by George! Reading Kalman's book-length testament is to experience happiness itself, so delightful are her often whimsical, brilliantly colored illustrations, which are accompanied by her sparer, hand-lettered text. Sprinkled throughout are photographs that offer a nicely realistic counterpoint to her stylized illustrations, which—like all her work—evoke the great artist Matisse. Some may call this a picture book; some, a graphic novel. But every reader will surely call it wonderful.

ANGELA'S ASHES

McCourt, Frank. Scribner, 1996. ISBN: 0684874350. **B/M**

Angela's Ashes is arguably one of the most celebrated memoirs in American literary history. McCourt is an amazing storyteller, and his memoir of growing up the eldest of eight children in Depression-era Ireland is beautifully and movingly told. With an alcoholic father and a depressed mother, it's no wonder the family lived in such poverty and squalor that three of McCourt's siblings died of complications from starvation. Despite the worst sort of privation, McCourt never lost his sense of humor and as an adult recalls his early years with tenderness and generosity of spirit. His memoir deservedly won virtually every major literary award in America, including the Pulitzer Prize, the National Book Critics Circle Award, and the *Los Angeles Times Book Prize*. This modern classic is indispensible reading for young adults and, indeed, for readers of all ages.

ANNE FRANK: THE BOOK, THE LIFE, THE AFTERLIFE

Prose, Francine. Harper, 2009. ISBN: 9780061430794. **B/M, HIST, LOI, GNF**

Novelist and discerning critic Prose offers a universally praised, innovative reexamination of Frank's *Diary of a Young Girl*, treating it as a "consciously crafted work of literature" as well as an inadvertent work of history. As might be expected, her analysis of the work is thoroughgoing, discerning, and thought-provoking, while her attention to the larger Anne Frank phenomenon that has grown up since *Diary*'s first publication is fascinating. Teachers will find her thoughtful attention to the use of *Diary* with students particularly helpful. A highly recommend and important book.

In *Reading like a Writer: A Guide for People Who Love Books and for Those Who Want to Write Them*, Prose writes persuasively of the necessary interrelationship between reading and writing, suggesting that the former is essential to the latter. In making her case she includes excerpts from master writers like Flannery O'Connor, Katherine Mansfield, Samuel Johnson, and more. How do you learn to write? First you read, read, read! Excellent advice, beautifully written and argued.

ARDENCY: A CHRONICLE OF THE *AMISTAD* REBELS

Young, Kevin. Knopf, 2011. ISBN: 9780307267641. **P, HIST, LOI**

Young, a celebrated poet and professor of English and creative writing at Emory University, has written a tribute, in verse, to the *Amistad* rebels, Africans who mutinied on the slave ship bringing them from Cuba to the New World. The mutiny was quickly put down and the Africans imprisoned, but their act of resistance has been an inspiration to all those seeking freedom ever since. Himself an African American, Young spent twenty years working on this poetic project, bringing remarkable dedication and a huge investment of self to it. Part of the book is written in the form of a libretto—entirely appropriate, since all of his language is like beautiful music.

AWKWARD AND DEFINITION / POTENTIAL / LIKEWISE

Schrag, Ariel. Simon & Schuster, 2008. ISBN: 9781416552314 / Touchstone, 2008. ISBN: 9781416552352 / Touchstone, 2009. ISBN: 9781416552376. **GN, B/M, LOI**

Originally self-published and created while she was still a student, Schrag's multivolume memoir is always candid and often funny and touching. *Awkward and Definition*, a compilation of the first two books in Schrag's original four-volume graphic novel, bring to vivid life Schrag's high school freshman and sophomore years in Berkeley, California, in the mid-'90s. *Potential* and *Likewise* record her junior and senior years, respectively. *Potential* also records her growing awareness of her homosexuality, which is dealt with candidly and more fully explored in *Likewise*. Schrag is particularly outspoken and visually explicit in dealing with her sexuality, which has caused some problems in libraries, but the book will undoubtedly strike a chord for teens questioning their sexuality as well as those who recognize themselves in the uncertainties and fears Schrag expresses.

BEAUTIFUL BOY

Sheff, David. Houghton Mifflin, 2008. ISBN: 9780618683352. **B/M**

Sheff, a journalist and contributing editor to *Playboy*, writes movingly about his son Nic's horrifying, decade-long addiction to methamphetamines and other drugs. As is often the case with addicts, it is as much Nic's seemingly willful recidivism, lies, and broken promises that are as painful to his family as his addiction. Worse, of course, is his willingness to do virtually anything to get drugs and the money to buy them, including stealing his 8-year-old brother's savings, living on the streets, breaking into the family home to steal, and on and on. So debilitating is his son's behavior that self-blaming Sheff is himself driven into therapy. Interestingly enough, the son, Nic, has written his own memoir of his addiction, *Tweak*, listed below.

BLANKETS
Thompson, Craig. Top Shelf, 2003. ISBN: 1891830430. **GN, B/M**

Thompson's award-winning graphic memoir is an extraordinarily ambitious autobiographical work, weighing in at 582 pages. The author/artist's efforts pay off as he creates a singularly successful and fascinating coming-of-age story, a large part of which is a tender story of first love. Born into a religious family in Wisconsin, Thompson also movingly recalls his difficult childhood and his ultimate loss of faith. *Blankets* has been hugely successful, winning two Eisners, three Harveys, and two Ignatz Awards. Thompson credits the fact that he didn't want "to do anything cynical and nihilistic, which is the standard for a lot of alternative comics." He brought the same generous sensibility to his earlier graphic novel, *Good-bye, Chunky Rice*.

THE BRIDGE: THE LIFE AND RISE OF BARACK OBAMA
Remnick, David. Knopf, 2010. ISBN: 9781400043606. **B/M**

Remnick, editor in chief of the *New Yorker*, has made a significant contribution to the literature about the forty-fourth president. In his exhaustively researched biography that focuses on Obama's life before his election to the presidency, Remnick proves the truth of the old cliché that "the child is father to the man." He seems to have talked to virtually everyone who was a factor in the making of the man, giving particular focus to Obama's quest, as a young person of mixed race, for community and of course—in the absence of his own—a viable father figure. There is much material here that has previously been unavailable, including a lengthy profile of that missing father. Smoothly written (Remnick calls it *biographical journalism*), the book gives special attention to Obama's role as a bridge between cultures—hence the title—and his life as a black man and community organizer. Indeed, Gwen Ifill, senior correspondent for PBS *News Hour*, praises Remnick for "not ducking the discussion of race and for peeling back several layers of the onion that is Barack Obama." Readers of this will also want to read the president's own two autobiographical works, *Dreams from My Father* and *The Audacity of Hope*. As for his mother, an excellent recent biography is Janny Scott's *A Singular Woman*.

BUTTERFLY BOY

González, Rigoberto. University of Wisconsin Press, 2006.

ISBN: 9780299219000. **B/M, LOI**

González's wrenching memoir of a first-generation Mexican American immigrant focuses on his growing up gay in a culture that finds that condition of being anathema. He recalls being beaten, for example, for wearing his mother's clothes and the social and familial opprobrium of being an overweight, bookish "mariposa." There are triumphs along the way, however: the son and grandson of migrant workers, he becomes the first in his family to graduate from high school. But that was only the beginning of his education, which has led to his being an associate professor of English and Latino studies at the University of Illinois. Readers of this book may well want to have a look at Richard Rodriguez's similar work, *Days of Obligation*.

THE *CALVIN AND HOBBES* TENTH ANNIVERSARY BOOK

Watterson, Bill. Andrews and McMeel, 1995. ISBN: 0836204409. **GN, HUM**

Speaking of comics, here is a generous collection of classic *Calvin and Hobbes* strips from the 1980s. The strips are accompanied by Watterson's invaluable commentary, which ranges from the origins of "Spaceman Spiff," Calvin's intergalactic alter ego, to the artist's strategy for creating stories. There are a number of other collections out there, but I've chosen this one for the sake of the commentary by this elusive artist (have you ever tried to find a picture of him?). Of course, serious fans will refuse to settle for anything less than the magnificent, gorgeously produced and printed three-volume *The Complete Calvin and Hobbes*. Yes, it costs $150, but it's worth every penny.

CANDYFREAK

Almond, Steve. Algonquin, 2004. ISBN: 1565124219. **B/M, HUM, ALEX**

Candy lovers, have I got a book for you! Here's a man—author Almond—who shares your passion, only in his case it's more like an obsession. In fact, he claims to have eaten a piece of candy every single day of his life! Consider this memoir, then, a real-life *Charlie and the Chocolate Factory*. Speaking of factories: Almond even goes on a road trip to tour some of these but finds, to his chagrin, that many candy manufacturers guard their secret ingredients nearly as jealously as the makers of Coca-Cola or the Colonel's chicken with its eleven secret herbs and spices. He has better luck with small regional manufacturers of such treats as Goldenberg's Peanut Chews, Goo Goo Clusters, and Idaho Spuds. Sweet!

COLUMBINE

Cullen, Dave. Twelve, 2009. ISBN: 9780446546935. **GNF**

Journalist Cullen has given readers by far the most complete account yet of the 1999 shootings that helped usher in a decade of similar school violence. He has combined countless interviews with a careful sifting of written documents and the paper and video trail left by the shooters Eric Harris and Dylan Klebold. In the process he debunks several prevailing myths—for example, the goth angle, the notion that specific students were targeted—but is relentless in his pursuit of the question why. To answer that he offers complex psychological profiles of the two teens, showing that Harris was a sadistic psychopath, and Klebold, an angry depressive. He also offers an in-depth look at the impact on the community, the school, and the students of the shootings. An invaluable book for those who are concerned about the spirit of violence that seems to be infecting our country.

COUNTING COUP

Colton, Larry. Warner, 2000. ISBN: 0446526835. **SPO, LOI, ALEX**

In Native American culture the term *counting coup* refers to winning prestige in battle by acts of bravery. In Colton's modern context it means performing well on the basketball court. A writer for *Sports Illustrated* and a former professional baseball player, Colton spent a year researching this book on the Crow Indian reservation in eastern Montana. His original plan was to write about the Hardin High School boys' basketball team, but instead he became fascinated by the girls' team, the Lady Bulldogs, and especially by the life of the team's Native American cocaptain, 17-year-old Sharon LaForge. He follows her life on and off the basketball court for a year and is even adopted into the tribe by her family. Nevertheless, he pulls no punches in describing the tensions between the white and Indian members of the team as well as investigating conditions on the reservation involving parental alcoholism and grinding poverty. Happy endings are elusive on the reservation, and Colton's conclusions are mixed, though LaForge's iron determination offers some hope for better days. A similar book that readers of *Counting Coup* will enjoy is *Eagle Blue* by Michael D'Orso, which is set in the remote Native American communities of the Alaskan bush. Like Colton, author D'Orso embedded himself in the community to record, in this case, the 2004–05 season of the Fort Yukon high school basketball team. Both were Alex Award choices.

THE DEVIL IN THE WHITE CITY

Larson, Erik. Crown, 2003. ISBN: 0609608444. **HIST**

The subtitle of Larson's epic work of narrative nonfiction—*Murder, Magic, and Madness at the Fair That Changed America*—may not tell the whole tale, but it certainly points readers wondering what this book is about in the right direction. The fair is the Chicago World's Fair of 1893, one of the most spectacular expositions of them all, thanks in large part to the architect and director of works Daniel Hudson Burnham, who was also responsible for New York's famous Flatiron Building and Union Station in Washington, DC. When Chicago was selected in 1890 as the prospective site, Burnham and his partner John Root brought aboard the participation of such other fabled talents as Frederick Law Olmsted, Louis Sullivan, and Richard M. Hunt. Despite this abundance of genius, the construction of "The White City" was not without its difficulties, among them inclement weather, labor unrest, a financial panic, and more. While Larson is vividly recreating this, he is also telling the parallel story of Dr. H. H. Holmes, a serial killer who built his World's Fair Hotel only a short distance away. The handsome doctor lured young women whom he then murdered in his "hotel," which was equipped with a gas chamber, a crematorium, and a vault in which he suffocated his victims. All of this and cameo appearances by the likes of Buffalo Bill, Susan B. Anthony, Thomas Edison, and others combine to make a nonfiction narrative that is as compulsively readable as an E. L. Doctorow novel.

DOONESBURY AND THE ART OF G. B. TRUDEAU

Walker, Brian. Yale University Press, 2010. ISBN: 9780300154276. **GN, HUM**

One of the great contemporary cartoonists gets his due in this definitive study of his art. Trudeau began drawing his sui generis comic strip in 1968 as a student at Yale. Two years later the strip went public, and now—more than forty years later—reaches an audience of some one hundred million. Walker examines Trudeau's creative process from inspiration to finished artwork and gives attention not only to the celebrated comic strip but also to Trudeau's other art, as well. His book is beautifully designed and generously illustrated with representative Trudeau strips. There is too little political literature for YAs, and *Doonesbury* provides an invaluable and highly accessible remedy for this. Walker—son of Mort Walker, creator of *Beetle Bailey*—is a highly regarded comics historian. Anyone with even a passing interest in this lively art form will enjoy Walker's piece de resistance *The Comics: The Complete Collection*, a compilation of his previous two volumes of comic strip history.

EAARTH: MAKING A LIFE ON A TOUGH NEW PLANET

McKibben, Bill. Times Books, 2010. ISBN: 9780805090567. **SCI**

One of America's finest and most influential writers on the environment, McKibben here wrestles with the issue of global warming. His amply supported premise is that Earth has been so changed by the depredations of global warming that it deserves a new name: the Eaarth of the title. And he makes such a compelling case for this that it seems incredible that there are still those who deny the phenomenon, which McKibben first described twenty years ago in his book *The End of Nature*. The author now feels that warming has reached a stage that cannot be reversed, but he offers thoughtful and cautiously optimistic recommendations for surviving its impact. To say that he simply calls for reducing the scale at which life is now excessively lived would be reductive and is only one of his partial solutions, another being the dramatic reduction of carbon emissions. For anyone who cares about the future of the planet—whether Earth or Eaarth—this is essential reading as, indeed, is McKibben's entire oeuvre.

EATING ANIMALS
Foer, Jonathan Safran. Little, Brown, 2009. ISBN: 9780316069908. **GNF**

The prospect of becoming a father was the catalyst for novelist Foer (see the entry for his *Extremely Loud and Incredibly Close*) to write this indictment of factory farms and other producers of meat for America's dining tables. Though an occasional vegetarian over the years, Foer remembers his grandmother's meat-included cooking with fondness, but his carefully documented investigation of modern methods of food production—including assembly line slaughter—is horrifying, especially when he turns his attention to animal intelligence, emotions, and capacity to feel pain. And Foer's definition of *animals* also includes fish. The author's first nonfiction book is compulsively readable and completely unforgettable. It's must reading for young adults who are considering their own diets and whether they should include meat. Chances are that more than one will choose to become a vegetarian or even a vegan after reading Foer.

THE *ENDURANCE*
Alexander, Caroline. Knopf, 1998. ISBN: 0375404031. **ADV, HIST, ALEX**

Beginning with Sebastian Junger's *The Perfect Storm* and Jon Krakauer's *Into Thin Air*, one of the most popular forms of adult nonfiction for YAs has been the adventure tale. There's nothing terribly mysterious about this: the nonfiction we're talking about here is narrative nonfiction, that is, a record of reality presented by using the tools of fiction writers. And what better, more suspenseful story is there than one of survival, whether it's contemporary or—like Alexander's story of the ill-fated 1914 Shackleton expedition to the South Pole—historic? Following the loss of their ship the *Endurance*, the crew of twenty-seven found themselves stranded in Antarctica for twenty-two months during which time they had to endure two-hundred-mile-per-hour winds and temperatures that plummeted to a hundred degrees below zero. With statistics like these, could anyone of the crew have survived? That, of course, is the question that will attract readers and keep them reading until the last page of this amazing story that Alexander has told with elegance and drama.

EPILEPTIC

B., David. Pantheon, 2005. ISBN: 0375423184. **GN, B/M**

First published in France, this memoir in graphic novel form recounts the author/artist's experience of growing up in the 1960s with an older brother, Jean-Christophe, who suffered from epilepsy. It is also the story of the family's years-long search for a cure, a search that takes them from medical science to such new age "remedies" as macrobiotic diets, mediums, acupuncturists, and more—sadly, all to no avail. The author—whose birth name is Pierre-François Beauchard—dealt with this and his fraught relationship with his brother by retreating into an elaborate fantasy world that he created in drawings that are an integral part of his narrative. Some American readers may be put off a bit by the very European sensibility evidenced here, and some may find the expressionist black-and-white art ugly, but it's hard to imagine anyone not being touched by their cumulative power. A founder of L'Association, a French comic artist collective, David B. is regarded as one of the world's greatest graphic artists, and *Publishers Weekly* has called this "one of the greatest graphic novels ever published." (The first half of this story was published in the United States in 2002. This edition contains both volumes.)

ESSENTIAL PLEASURES:
A NEW ANTHOLOGY OF POEMS TO READ ALOUD

Pinsky, Robert, ed. Norton, 2009. ISBN: 9780393066081. **P**

The former poet laureate assembles a generous (528-page) collection of poems that lend themselves to being read aloud. Arranged by type of poem—narrative, love poems, odes, parodies, and so on—the collection spans centuries and contains both familiar poems and ones that will be new to all but the most expert readers. A CD of Pinksy reading the poems is included and may be illuminating to those who are novices at oral interpretation. For librarians who use poetry in programming, this is an essential purchase. Consider this in concert with Mark Eleveld's *The Spoken Word Revolution*. During his term as America's poet laureate, Pinsky started his Favorite Poem Project, inviting Americans to submit their favorite poem. A number of these were then selected to be read by the person who submitted them; the readings were videotaped for inclusion in a new national archive. This anthology collects many of those poems. What sets it apart from other anthologies is that each poem is introduced with an essay by its submitter, who explains the significance of the poem to him or her. The results, published in *Americans' Favorite Poems: The Favorite Poem Project Anthology*, are sometimes surprising, often heart-warming, and always uniquely insightful. It's an excellent complement to the anthology above.

EVERY LIVING THING

Herriot, James. St. Martin's, 1992. ISBN: 031208188X. **B/M**

In the same vein as his modern classic *All Creatures Great and Small*, the British veterinarian shares more recollections of his life work with animals in the 1950s. This fifth and final memoir (Herriot died in 1995 at the age of 79) is every bit as touching and involving as the first four and is required reading for animal lovers everywhere. (Thanks to the international success of his books and the BBC dramatization of the first, Herriot became a cultural phenomenon, and fans may be interested to know there is a World of James Herriot Museum in Thirsk, North Yorkshire.) Other titles by Herriot include *All Things Bright and Beautiful*, *All Things Wise and Wonderful*, and *The Lord God Made Them All*.

FAST FOOD NATION: THE DARK SIDE
OF THE ALL-AMERICAN MEAL

Schlosser, Eric. Houghton Mifflin, 2001. ISBN: 0395977894. **GNF**

Atlantic Monthly correspondent Schlosser offers a definitive and often disturbing look at America's unhealthy love affair with fast food and the burgeoning industry that feeds the habit. From the inhumane breeding of animals on factory farms to the exploitation of workers—the largest share of them being teenagers—to an in-depth profile of McDonald's to an examination of chemically enhanced flavors, Schlosser offers an investigative reporter's indictment of an industry that many reviewers have rightly pointed out evokes Upton Sinclair's pioneer muckraking works, especially his exposé of the meatpacking industry, *The Jungle*. Schlosser's book was turned into a 2006 fictional film directed by Richard Linklater and starring Greg Kinnear.

FIST STICK KNIFE GUN

Canada, Geoffrey, and Jamar Nicholas. Beacon, 2010.

ISBN: 9780807044490. **GN, B/M**

Author Canada—founder of the widely praised Harlem Children's Zone—grew up in the South Bronx in the 1950s when violence was an integral part of childhood. His careful examination of the strata of physical violence notes its seemingly inexorable movement from fists to sticks to knives to—ultimately—guns, and shows how such weapons became part of everyday life . . . and death. Canada's memoir of his early life—first published in 1995 (still available from Beacon)—has now been turned into an exceptional graphic novel by the artist Jamar Nicholas. His addition of art to a (necessarily) abridged text brings a visceral immediacy and a visually powerful context to the still urgently important text. The availability of these two different but linked versions of the same book should greatly expand its potential readership.

FUN HOME: A FAMILY TRAGICOMIC

Bechdel, Alison. Houghton Mifflin, 2006. ISBN: 0618477942. **GN, B/M**

The subtitle, *A Family Tragicomic*, speaks volumes about this quite brilliant graphic novel. It promises and proceeds to deliver in spades. Bechdel's father was a third-generation mortician, and she and her brothers grew up calling the funeral parlor the "Fun Home." And, yes, this was ironic, for there was not much that could be described as "fun" about the cult cartoonist's childhood (she's the creator of the comic strip *Dykes to Watch Out For*, which has been in publication since 1983). Much of the book is devoted to her fraught relationship with her father, who—in addition to being a mortician—was an obsessive restorer of the family's huge Gothic revival house. Bechdel's childhood friends called it a mansion, but to her and her brothers it was just a home. It was definitely not where the heart was, for Bechdel's parents had a troubled relationship largely because Bechdel's father was not only emotionally remote but also a closeted homosexual, who had clandestine relationships with his students and even with the family's male babysitter. Of course Bechdel didn't know this at the time. Nor did she know that she herself was a lesbian until much later. Bechdel describes her childhood as "a still life with children." Readers of her outspoken memoir will be grateful she broke the silence. *Fun Home* received the prestigious Eisner Award in the category Best Reality-Based Work. It was also a finalist for the National Book Critics Circle Award.

GEEKS: HOW TWO LOST BOYS
RODE THE INTERNET OUT OF IDAHO

Katz, Jon. Villard, 2000. ISBN: 037550298X. **TECH**

Computer geeks rule, as Katz, a writer for *Rolling Stone* and *Wired* magazines, discovered when he devoted his column on Slashdot (http://slashdot.org) to the subject and received thousands of e-mails in response, most of them from young kids who had been branded "geeks" and subjected to teasing, tormenting and worse. Katz was particularly intrigued by an e-mail from a 19-year-old young man living in rural Idaho. Named Jesse Dailey, he and a friend, Eric Twilegar, repaired computers for a living but felt woefully out of place and misunderstood in their environment. Intrigued, Katz traveled to Idaho to meet them and then decided to write about them at the same time the two decided to move to Chicago in search of better lives. Katz chronicles their efforts while also writing about the larger world of geek culture and its societal implications. In the meantime he became a mentor for the boys, encouraging them and helping in whatever ways he could. His story assumes a dramatic urgency when—during its writing—the Columbine shootings took place and America became aware of outsiders and the bullying to which they are often subjected. Selected as a Best Book for Young Adults, this is a compelling read and an important book for YAs who need their consciousness raised.

GOOGLED: THE END OF THE WORLD AS WE KNOW IT

Auletta, Ken. Penguin, 2009. ISBN: 9781594202353. **TECH**

Based on extensive research and countless interviews and allowing for a certain degree of titular hyperbole, *New Yorker* media columnist Auletta writes a thoughtful history and penetrating analysis of one of the world's most important media companies. Begun as an Internet search engine by Larry Page and Sergey Brin when they were Stanford graduate students, Google has become vastly more—a digital empire that generates more than $20 billion in ad revenue annually. As Google grows, Auletta notes, it expands into all areas of traditional media—newspapers, publishing, movies, television, and more—both in the United States and internationally. Will it become a universal portal to all the world's knowledge? Perhaps. Certainly if it can overcome copyright issues, its controversial book digitization project could offer that hitherto elusive dream, a universal library. As Google continues to change the world of information, its impact on today's young adults and those of tomorrow will be enormous, and accordingly, this book makes for imperatively important reading.

HIGH EXPOSURE

Breashears, David. Simon & Schuster, 1999. ISBN: 0684853612. **ADV, ALEX**

The author is not only an avid mountain climber but also a celebrated, four-time Emmy Award–winning cinematographer. It was his latter role that took him to Mount Everest in 1996 to make the IMAX film *Everest* that later became another award winner. Coincidentally the author and his crew were at Everest when a devastating storm at its summit took eight lives, a tragic accident about which Jon Krakauer writes in his celebrated book *Into Thin Air*. Though Breashears escaped exposure to this particular storm, he has had many other adventurous experiences—some of them near fatal—climbing the world's mountains. What compels people to risk their lives in pursuit of peaks? Breashears admits he can't answer that question. Perhaps, in the final analysis, the reason for climbing a mountain, no matter how forbidding, is, simply, the familiar "Because it's there." Readers of Breashears's fascinating memoir will decide that for themselves.

I AM AN EMOTIONAL CREATURE:
THE SECRET LIFE OF GIRLS AROUND THE WORLD

Ensler, Eve. Villard, 2010. ISBN: 9781400061044. **GNF**

In a collection of dramatic monologues, the author and playwright (*The Vagina Monologues*) gives voices to teenage girls from all over the world. Employing a variety of literary forms ranging from poetry to blog entries, Ensler writes powerfully of such issues as genital mutilation, arranged marriages, anorexia, sex, and more. Her work is insightful, searing, and deeply emotional. Here she is, for example, on materialism: "What happened to not showing off your wealth? / What happened to kindness? / What happened to teenagers rebelling / Instead of buying and selling?" Ensler has an extraordinary capacity for finding the heart of an issue and casting it in emotional terms that will acquaint older teens with their own capacity to feel and to understand the heartbreaking plights of other teenage girls from around the world.

I SHALL NOT BE MOVED

Angelou, Maya. Random House, 1991. ISBN: 9780553354584. **P, LOI**

Arguably best known to YAs for her powerful memoir *I Know Why the Caged Bird Sings*, Angelou is also a gifted poet, as she evidences in this fifth collection of her work. Though she writes in a variety of poetic forms, she brings a common element of lyricism and grace to her often moving poems about the black experience. Their inherent drama is further testimony to the fact that in addition to being a poet and a memoirist, Angelou is a performer, and hearing her read her own work is a revelation. Students will also enjoy vocally interpreting these poems.

THE ICE MASTER

Niven, Jennifer. Hyperion, 2000. ISBN: 0786865296. **ADV, HIST**

Niven tells the story of the ill-fated voyage of the ship *Karluk*. Setting off from British Columbia in 1913 as part of a journey of discovery organized by the explorer Vilhjalmur Stefansson on behalf of the Canadian government, the trip soon sours when the ship becomes trapped by pack ice and sinks in January 1914. While the *Karluk* is still afloat, Stefansson and five others leave the ship to "go hunting," though there is a body of opinion that they simply abandoned the ship and its remaining crew, whose struggle to survive ends in the death of eleven. In retrospect, it is obvious that the ship should never have set sail. Its captain, Robert Bartlett, had grave reservations about its seaworthiness from the beginning, and its chief engineer, John Munro, described its engine as "a coffee pot never intended to run more than two days at a time." Unfortunately Stefansson overruled them, and the result was a disaster. Niven is a screenwriter, and she has brought her expertise to a cinematic and dramatic account of this sad story.

THE IMMORTAL LIFE OF HENRIETTA LACKS

Skloot, Rebecca. Crown, 2010. ISBN: 9781400052172. **B/M, TECH, LOI**

The "immortal" of the title refers to the cells of the eponymous Lacks, an African American woman who was admitted to the Johns Hopkins Hospital in 1951 suffering from cervical cancer. Without her knowledge or permission, doctors took tissue samples from her cervix and used them to create the first "immortal" cell line, named HeLa. These cells were widely used in medical research that led to the discovery—among others—of the polio vaccine. The sale of her cells over the years generated millions of dollars in income, none of which the Lacks family saw. Skloot's story is the result of some ten years of research during which she became close to the Lacks family, especially Lacks's daughter Deborah. Not only is the story one of injustice, poverty, and racial discrimination, it is also—more positively—the story of the creation of the field of bioethics, an important advance in the field of medicine. Despite its complexities the book is accessibly and vividly written and, in parts, reads like a combination of fiction and investigative journalism.

IN THE HEART OF THE SEA
Philbrick, Nathaniel. Viking, 2000. ISBN: 0670891576. **ADV, HIST, ALEX**

Philbrick, director of the Egan Institute of Maritime Studies, has written a dramatic account of yet another ill-fated voyage, this one of the whaler *Essex*, which inspired Melville's *Moby Dick*. Leaving its home port of Nantucket in 1819, it reaches the South Seas when it's sunk after a sperm whale rams it. Its twenty crew members take to three small whaleboats and drift for more than ninety days. So short of rations are they that some resort to cannibalism to survive. When finally rescued off the coast of Chile, only five are left alive. Subsequently three more are found alive on a small island. The third boat vanishes and has never been found. As Sebastian Junger did with *The Perfect Storm*, Philbrick has brought a disastrous sea voyage to vivid life while also giving considerable attention to its home port. Philbrick's book, a real contribution to maritime history, received the National Book Award.

INTO THIN AIR: A PERSONAL
ACCOUNT OF THE MT. EVEREST DISASTER
Krakauer, Jon. Villard, 1997. ISBN: 0679457526. **ADV, ALEX**

The disaster in question took place in the spring of 1996. On assignment from *Outside* magazine, journalist Krakauer joined a commercial expedition that was scheduled to guide novice climbers to Everest's 29,000-foot peak. Though the mountain has been conquered numerous times since 1953 when Sir Edmund Hillary and his Sherpa guide Tenzing Norgay became the first to accomplish the feat, advances in equipment and climbing techniques in the years since have somewhat diminished the perils involved in the undertaking. Nevertheless, Krakauer wondered, is it safe for tour companies to guide wealthy but inexperienced mountaineers to the peak? (Anyone willing to part with $65,000 can make the ascent!) As the reader learns, the answer is a resounding no. Even Krakauer, a skilled climber, found extreme difficulties once the expedition reached the mountain's so-called dead zone at 25,000 feet. Such an extreme altitude can cause disorientation and muscular disorders. For Krakauer it was as if his blood had turned to sludge and his extremities to wood. Nevertheless the group pressed on until the day they were to reach the summit. Then, out of nowhere, a violent storm caught the group. Krakauer managed to escape but eight others died, including two of the best climbers in the world. Clearly Everest, "the goddess of the sky," remains a force to be reckoned with.

Krakauer's book is one of two (the other being Junger's *The Perfect Storm*) that were largely responsible for ushering in the new age of narrative nonfiction. Though still nonfiction (reality is not manipulated), this form borrows narrative techniques from fiction writing. Krakauer's book is a perfect example of this technique in action and remains a model to this day. *Into the Wild*, another book by Krakauer, runs a close second to *Into Thin Air* in popularity, especially since a major motion picture version starring Emile Hirsch and directed by Sean Penn was released in 2007. Krakauer's book and the movie based on it tell the story of a young man named Chris McCandless who set off to test himself against the Alaskan wilderness. Captivated by the writings of Tolstoy and Thoreau, McCandless, after graduating from Emory University, left his possessions behind, donated his entire savings of $24,000 to charity, and hitchhiked to Alaska, vanishing into the wilderness. Four months later he was found dead of starvation. Does he deserve the reader's sympathy or is the fault one of his own hubris, inexperience, and ignorance of wilderness survival? And why did he undertake such an impossible mission in the first place? These are questions that Krakauer attempts to answer as he unfolds this fascinating story. Like *Into Thin Air*, this title is highly recommended and is sure to be a classic of nature writing.

JESUS LAND

Scheeres, Julia. Counterpoint, 2005. ISBN: 1582433380. **B/M, ALEX, LOI**

Journalist Scheeres grew up in Indiana in the 1970s, and it was there that one day she and one of her two adopted black brothers see a sign proudly proclaiming "This Here Is JESUS LAND." And so it certainly is for her family, thanks to her devout parents. Religion is also omnipresent at her school, but it does not save her and her brothers from vile expressions of racial prejudice. In fact there is almost no expression of love in the pious protests of the self-styled religious who surround her. To backslide from the ordained order is to receive a stiff punishment. In Scheeres's case and that of her brother David, that means being sent off to a fundamentalist reform school in the Dominican Republic, where punishment and humiliation of various sorts are the order of the day. Somehow Scheeres manages to distance herself from these bitter experiences and recalls them with remarkable equanimity, which is—come to think of it—a far more sincere expression of religion than any she experienced growing up.

JOHNNY CASH: I SEE A DARKNESS

Kleist, Reinhard. Abrams, 2009. ISBN: 9780810984639. **GN, B/M**

This graphic novel biography of American singer Johnny Cash by a German author/artist is a multiple award winner in Europe. As is appropriate for a book about the Man in Black, Kleist's treatment, both in text and art, is tinged with darkness as he limns the singer's life from childhood to midcareer success (a flash forward brings the story up to Cash's last years as he selects songs for his American Recordings series). Kleist pulls no punches as he examines Cash's troubles with drugs and the disintegration of his first marriage. But he also pays appropriate tribute to one of the greatest musicians of the twentieth century. What is truly remarkable about this book, however, is how a German has managed to capture the essence of this quintessentially American singer/songwriter/performer.

KAMPUNG BOY / TOWN BOY

Lat. First Second, 2006. ISBN: 1596431210 / First Second, 2007.
ISBN: 1596433310. **GN, LOI, HUM**

This two-volume graphic novel memoir recalls the Malaysian cartoonist's childhood growing up in the 1960s. The first volume focuses on his early life in a small village (*kampung*); the second, on his teen years at a boarding school in town. Both volumes are distinguished by their affectionate humor, gift for caricature, and capacity for capturing universal coming-of-age experiences.

Lat's black-and-white illustrations are a delight, often laugh-out-loud funny and affectionately nostalgic. While the experiences may be foreign to Western readers, the spirit of mischief (telling the 'rents you're going to the library and going instead to the local arcade) is universal. The books also demonstrate the universality of the comics medium and its ability to cut across cultural and geographic boundaries.

THE LAST BOY: MICKEY MANTLE
AND THE END OF AMERICA'S CHILDHOOD

Leavy, Jane. Harper, 2010. ISBN: 9780060883522. **B/M, SPO**

There have been other biographies of the late baseball icon, but none as good as this one. It's a sad story that Leavy tells about the disconnect between popular image and reality. The product of prodigious research—the author conducted more than five hundred interviews—Leavy's in-depth portrait handily demonstrates that baseball fans during Mantle's legendary career refused to acknowledge any truth that was at variance with the player's heroic image. In fact, the reality was far from the legend. Mantle was an alcoholic, verbally abusive to his family, and a serial womanizer. Growing up a devoted fan, Leavy became a sportswriter for the *Washington Post* and twice interviewed her childhood "hero," an opportunity that brought home the unfortunate truth about Mantle the person. In today's celebrity-ridden, tell-all culture, it's hard to believe that there was a time so innocent that such a deeply flawed human being could have attained Mantle's legendary status, but it was, as Leavy demonstrates, just such a time. Hers is a cautionary tale that invites young readers to develop critical thinking and to question the tropes of popular culture. Leavy is also the author of acclaimed biography *Sandy Koufax: A Lefty's Legacy*, an excellent book to read in concert with *The Last Boy*, for while Koufax attained the same degree of celebrity, he was a model of integrity in his private life, a too rare case where legend and reality actually coincided.

LOGICOMIX: AN EPIC SEARCH FOR TRUTH

Doxiadis, Apostolos, and Christos H. Papadimitriou.
Bloomsbury, 2009. ISBN: 9781596914520. **GN, B/M**

The truth being sought here is the logical foundation of mathematics, and the searcher is the late British mathematician/philosopher Bertrand Russell, whose biography in graphic novel form this is. The coauthors are themselves philosophers but bring an accessible style and strategy to their intellectually stimulating story. It begins with a celebrated speech by Russell in which he expresses his well-known pacifist ideas that are then a catalyst for the flashback that will recount his lifelong quest. In an intriguingly metafictional way the coauthors bring themselves and others into a frame story that discusses Russell and his colleagues and the taint of insanity that visited so many of their lives. This is a superbly original graphic novel that demonstrates the flexibility of the form and the capacity of text and drawings to interact to make even abstruse material accessible. (It should be noted that I could have placed this book in the fiction section, since the authors acknowledge some fudging of facts. But the essential theme, supporting incidents, and ideas are sufficiently factual that I decided to place it here.)

A LONG WAY GONE

Beah, Ishmael. Farrar Straus Giroux, 2007. ISBN: 9780374105235. **B/M, LOI, ALEX**

Beah's memoir tells the horrifying story of how, when he was 12, rebels invaded his hometown in Sierra Leone, and separated from his parents, he began a ghastly life of wandering until he was recruited into the military and—equipped with an AK-47 rifle and fed a diet of amphetamines—was turned into a killing machine along with other young boys his age. For three years he participated in the slaughter of rebels in Sierra Leone's ongoing civil war. Fortunately he was saved from this life by the United Nations and, after a period of rehabilitation, was chosen to address the United Nations in New York. When he was 17, he managed to move to this country permanently, graduating from Oberlin College in 2004.

Washington Post book critic Carolyn See has said, "Everyone in the world should read this book. We should read it to learn about the world and about what it means to be human." And there is no arguing with this assessment, whether the reader is an adult or a young adult.

LOUISA MAY ALCOTT: THE WOMAN BEHIND *LITTLE WOMEN*

Reisen, Harriet. Holt, 2009. ISBN: 9780805082999. **B/M, HIST**

Reading Alcott's most famous novel has been a rite of passage for American girls since the book's publication in 1868. But what of the woman who wrote it? Readers will find the fascinating answer here in a book that grew out the author's research for her screenplay of the first television documentary about Alcott, an episode of the PBS series American Masters. Alcott was the daughter of the educator and philosopher Bronson Alcott, a brilliant man who was nevertheless totally unequipped to deal with the practicalities of the world. This visited enormous hardship on his wife, Abigail, the Marmee of the highly autobiographical *Little Women*. It also meant that Louisa had, of necessity, to become the family breadwinner—which, happily, she was able to do through her writing, not only her half-dozen children's books but also through her highly successful potboilers, all written either anonymously or pseudonymously. Her childhood and young adult years in Concord, Massachusetts, make for fascinating reading, as the Alcotts were close friends of Ralph Waldo Emerson (who often provided financial assistance to them), Henry David Thoreau (upon whom Alcott had a crush), Nathaniel Hawthorne, and other luminaries. As a protofeminist Alcott was clearly years ahead of her time and remains an example to young women to this day. There are a number of other good biographies of Alcott; one of the best of these is John Matteson's *Eden's Outcasts: The Story of Louisa May Alcott and Her Father*.

MAKES ME WANNA HOLLER:
A YOUNG BLACK MAN IN AMERICA

McCall, Nathan. Random House, 1994. ISBN: 0679412689. **ALEX, B/M, LOI**

Now a lecturer in the Department of African American Studies at Emory University, McCall was a reporter for the *Washington Post* when he wrote this angry memoir-cum-commentary on black male life in America. Born in poverty in Virginia, McCall grew up to be sentenced to twelve years in prison for armed robbery. Working as prison librarian, he discovered and was inspired by the work of black novelist and essayist Richard Wright. After being released, McCall completed his education determined to become a writer. He was subsequently hired by the *Post*. Replete with rape, drugs, guns, robbery, and racial prejudice that sometimes segues into outright hatred, McCall's memoir is a harrowing read. Perhaps most disturbing is his assertion that serving time in prison has become a rite of passage for young black men. Selected as an Alex Award winner, *Makes Me Wanna Holler* has been popular with teens since its publication and is still relevant to studies of race and culture in America.

ME TALK PRETTY ONE DAY

Sedaris, David. Little, Brown, 2000. ISBN: 9780316777728. **HUM**

Though obviously edgier, Sedaris's hilarious personal essays may remind older readers of the late Robert Benchley, who, like Sedaris, was a master of self-deprecating humor and whose essays published in the 1920s, '30s, and '40s are still as fresh and clever as they were when newly minted. One suspects Sedaris will have equal staying power. Any one of his collections could have been featured here, but this one, which finds Sedaris and his boyfriend Hugh moving to France, is a particular favorite with YAs. The title is a reference to Sedaris's awkward attempts to learn French, which advance haltingly, from his speaking "like an evil baby to speaking like a hillbilly." No wonder his frustrated teacher acidly tells him, "Every day spent with you is like having a cesarean section." As always, when Sedaris isn't taking potshots at himself, his targets of choice are his family. In this volume it's the author's father, Lou, who is the principal target, but his mother also appears on the firing line. In fact his entire family have so often been in his crosshairs, it's a wonder they haven't sued him for contempt of clan, but one suspects they're too busy laughing to file suit. The reader certainly is.

NAME ALL THE ANIMALS

Smith, Alison. Scribner, 2004. ISBN: 0743255224. **B/M**

In 1984 when the author was only 15, her beloved 18-year-old brother was killed in an automobile accident. This touching and beautifully written memoir tells the story of how she and her family coped with this monumental loss. Devout Catholics, Smith's parents find solace in their religion, but the author has less success, losing her faith and trying to find it in questioning how and why this tragedy could happen. Blaming herself, she begins acting out both at home, slipping out in the middle of the night, and also at her Catholic high school; but her teacher nuns excuse rather than confront her behavior. More seriously she becomes secretly anorexic, though no one seems to notice her alarming weight loss (or if they do, they fail to comment or act). Smith subsequently enters a "forbidden" love relationship with another girl. It being the 1980s blame has to be assigned when the relationship is discovered, and it is the other girl who bears the brunt. As the third anniversary of her brother's death looms, Smith even considers suicide. Will she find healing and redemption?

NEEDLES

Dominick, Andie. Scribner, 1997. ISBN: 0684842327. **B/M, ALEX**

When the author was 9, she was diagnosed with diabetes. The disease was no stranger to her, however, since her older sister also suffered from it. Indeed, when Andie was a little girl, she and brother were in the habit of playing with their sister's discarded needles! The sister, Denise, brought a degree of normalcy to Andie's new life that was otherwise controlled by her disease. Unfortunately, as Denise grew older, she began using cocaine and otherwise neglecting her health. As a result, she died when she was 33, and it was Andie who discovered her body. Dominick spares her readers no details of the grittier aspects of her own diabetes, writing about the details of her daily injections, her necessary eye surgeries, her abortion when she became pregnant at 17, and, when she married, her decision to have a tubal ligation to avoid passing on her disease to any children she might have had. Clearly this is not a happy story but an important one, and like many nonfiction accounts of illnesses, this book has had a large readership among teens.

NICKLE AND DIMED

Ehrenreich, Barbara. Holt, 2002. ISBN: 0805063889. **GNF, ALEX**

Is it any longer possible to survive in America earning only the minimum wage? Social critic and journalist Ehrenreich decided to find out, and between 1998 and 2000, she spent approximately three months living in three different states (Minnesota, Florida, and Maine) working as an unskilled laborer, taking jobs as a Wal-Mart "associate," a nursing home aide, a cleaning woman, a hotel maid, and a waitress. Earning $7 an hour or approximately $300 per week, she quickly discovered the answer is no—especially in her case, since she refused any government assistance in the form of food stamps, Medicaid, or housing subsidies. Luckier than most, since she has no children to support and is in good health, she still found herself routinely working two jobs and living in rundown motels or trailer parks. Many of her coworkers, she discovered, were living in their cars and—like her—working seven days a week without any time off. Working conditions were deplorable: unskilled workers are constantly supervised because they are not trusted; they are discouraged from communicating with one another because talking on the job is regarded as "time theft"; and they are routinely victims of verbal abuse. Worst of all, Ehrenreich writes, is that the working poor are essentially invisible to middle- and upper-class Americans who barely recognize their humanity. This is an important (and highly readable) book that many young adults have embraced and that all of them need to read to understand enduring problems of class and poverty in America.

THE NORTON ANTHOLOGY OF LATINO LITERATURE

Stavans, Ilan, ed. Norton, 2010. ISBN: 9780393080070. **GNF, LOI**

Booklist called this a "keystone" collection and no wonder, for it includes 201 entries gathered from over five centuries of writing from Latino/ Spanish-speaking countries. In so doing it dramatically demonstrates the diversity of cultures and traditions that inform this world—then and now. At a time when the Latino population in America is burgeoning, this is an invaluable collection that will introduce teens—and adults—to a culture rich in tradition and art. Consider it especially important in the continuing absence of any significant body of Latino literature published for young adult readers. In *Spanglish*, another book of interest to YAs, Stavans, the Lewis-Sebring Professor in Latin American and Latino Culture at Amherst College, has written an illuminating study of the newly hybrid language that has emerged from the growing encounters between Spanish and English (the two most widely spoken languages in the United States)—and between Latino and Anglo cultures and traditions. Much of the fascinating study in linguistics is devoted to an invaluable lexicon of more than two thousand terms; equally intriguing is the author's exemplary translation of the first chapter of *Don Quixote* into Spanglish. *Spanglish* is an important work that can be used in concert with the *Norton Anthology* above. Though controversial among linguistic purists, Spanglish may be the language of the future as the Latino population of America continues to grow.

ONE HUNDRED DEMONS

Barry, Lynda. Sasquatch Books, 2005. ISBN: 9781570614590.

GN, B/M, HUM, ALEX

"Is it autobiography if parts of it are not true? Is it fiction if parts of it are?" Barry asks in the introduction to this generous collection of twenty cartoon stories that first appeared in the e-zine *Salon*'s Mothers Who Think department. The answer from most of her readers will be, "Who cares? Just get on with the stories," which she does. And all have her signature mix of the poignant and the briskly humorous. What further connects them are their subjects: each one is about a personal demon, ranging from head lice to dancing, from hate to magic, from cicadas to dogs, and more. Each successive cartoon panel is filled with her hand-lettered text and her wonderfully idiosyncratic and sui generis expressionist cartoons. While the content comes directly from her past, Barry acknowledges in her introduction that the concept came from a book she found at the library (yeah!). It was about a painting exercise called, yes, "One Hundred Demons," and one example of the inspiration it offered was a hand scroll painted by a Zen monk named Hakuin Ekaku in sixteenth-century Japan. An appendix shows demon-ridden readers how to paint their own demons. "Come on!" Barry concludes. "Don't you want to try it?"

PACKING FOR MARS:
THE CURIOUS SCIENCE OF LIFE IN THE VOID

Roach, Mary. Norton, 2010. ISBN: 9780393068474. **TECH, SCI, HUM**

Roach, a journalist with a gift for the offbeat, tackles the life of astronauts in space, giving her readers a sometimes comic but always informative take on the subject. How, for example, are bodily functions handled in space? What about space sickness? What's it like to be weightless? (She finds out herself by taking a parabolic flight on a McDonnell Douglas C-9.) The author has treated her subject with her customary wit and spirit and has seemingly covered every aspect of her sometimes challenging—and queasy-making—subject. Indeed, the book might well have been subtitled *Everything You Didn't Know You Wanted to Know about Physical Life in Space*. It's a terrific read.

Although this book was, surprisingly, not an Alex Award selection, Roach's earlier book *Stiff: The Curious Lives of Human Cadavers* was an Alex choice. In it the author demonstrates that what happens to human corpses shouldn't happen to a (dead) dog! Shall we say that cadavers simply get no respect? They're decapitated for use in plastic surgery education, used as test dummies, and—of course—employed (talk about cheap labor) in medical research and experimentation. The author's research included interviewing a whole host of people who use cadavers in various ways. While Roach treats her subject with respect, she also enlivens it with the occasional zinger: being a cadaver is like being on a cruise ship—"you spend most of your time flat on your back."

THE PERFECT STORM

Junger, Sebastian. Norton, 1997. ISBN: 9780393337013. **ADV, ALEX**

Junger's breathtaking account of the Halloween Gale of October 1991—the "perfect storm" of the title—was one of the first popular contemporary examples of what is called *narrative nonfiction*; that is, nonfiction whose author employs the tools of the novelist as did Truman Capote in his modern classic *In Cold Blood*. Like Capote, Junger focuses on the human aspect of the story, giving particular attention to the captain and crew of the fishing boat the *Andrea Gail* that was lost with all hands in the devastating storm. Junger's account of what the experience of the storm, with its 110-foot waves and 120-mile-per-hour winds, must have been like is breathtakingly suspenseful, as is his further account of another boat—a sailboat—also caught in the storm and the dramatic rescue of its crew by the Coast Guard. In the wake of the storm he returns to the ship's home port, Gloucester, Massachusetts, to gauge its residents' responses to the tragedy, adding a further human element to his story. Along with Jon Krakauer's *Into Thin Air*, this book also began the current trend in crossover adult books for young adults.

In *War*, Junger, whose writing career seems to be constantly putting him in harm's way, writes about the fifteen-month period during which he was embedded with a U.S. Army unit, the Second Platoon, Battle Company, in the Korengal Valley of eastern Afghanistan. This example of immersion journalism offers readers an up close and personal view of some of the heaviest fighting in Afghanistan, and Junger was present every step of the way, even surviving an IED attack that blew up the Humvee in which he was riding. The best part of the book, however, is not the action—though there's plenty of that—but rather Junger's empathetic portraits of the unit's members and his larger considerations of the nature of combat and its psychological and emotional impact on those involved.

PERSEPOLIS / PERSEPOLIS 2

Satrapi, Marjane. Pantheon, 2003. ISBN: 0375422307 / Pantheon, 2004.
ISBN: 0375422889. **GN, B/M, ALEX, LOI**

In this two-volume memoir in graphic novel form, Satrapi, who was born in 1969, vividly recreates her childhood in Iran during the period of the fall of the Shah—to whom her family is distantly related—and the Islamic revolution that followed. Life under a fundamentalist government is radically different than here in the United States, especially for women, and Satrapi has considerable difficulty adapting. Indeed, her rebellious streak endangers her family to the degree that when she is 14, she is sent to study in Europe. Volume 2 continues this story, recounting her four-year education in Vienna. Problems of culture shock and assimilation end with Satrapi living on the streets and, as a result, returning to Iran. There she makes an unfortunate marriage but, more fortunately, goes to art school. Ultimately her marriage ends, and the still outspoken and rebellious Satrapi returns to Europe and ultimately settles in France, where these two books were first published to great critical acclaim. Satrapi's black-and-white drawings might best be described as expressionistic, though some have called them faux naive. Whichever, they provide a perfect complement to her memorable text.

THE PHOTOGRAPHER

Guibert, Emmanuel, Didier Lefèvre and Frédéric Lemercier.
First Second, 2009. ISBN: 9781596433755. **GN, ADV**

In 1986—during the Afghan war with Russia—the French photojournalist Lefèvre traveled to a remote region of northern Afghanistan to join a team of Doctors Without Borders. His record of the subsequent three-month period he spent in their company is contained in his extraordinary black-and-white photographs, which comprise part of the visual content of this mixed medium work. The other part is found in Guibert's realistic cartoons. As is normally the case, text is either contained in speech balloons or as captions to the images. The combination of all three elements heighten the reality and the visceral impact of the reader's experience. Published in three volumes in Europe, this collaborative effort has sold more than a quarter of a million copies there. It is, as *Booklist* magazine said, "a magnificent achievement."

THE RADIOACTIVE BOY SCOUT

Silverstein, Ken. Random House, 2004. ISBN: 037550351X. **TECH**

Silverstein, an investigative reporter for the *Los Angeles Times*, tells the remarkable story of a suburban Detroit teenager named David Hahn. Working on his Boy Scout atomic energy badge in the early 1990s, Hahn became fascinated with nuclear energy and decided to build a model nuclear reactor in his backyard. Posing as a physicist, he was able to garner much of the necessary information to build a reactor. Using blueprints from an old physics book he managed to make significant progress toward his goal until the experiment began emitting enough radiation to jeopardize the entire population of his hometown—at which point the Environmental Protection Agency was alerted and took away the lab to be buried at a nuclear waste dump in Utah. Who says American enterprise is dead?

RATS: OBSERVATIONS ON THE HISTORY AND HABITAT OF THE CITY'S MOST UNWANTED INHABITANTS

Sullivan, Robert. Bloomsbury, 2004. ISBN: 1582343853. **GNF, ALEX, HIST, B/M**

Not surprisingly, the "city" of the title is New York, where the rat population has been estimated at as high as eight million. In the interest of fairness, however, some have also estimated it as low as 250,000. In either case, it's a whole lot of rats! Based on a *Talk of the Town* piece he wrote for the *New Yorker* magazine, Sullivan's up-close and personal look at the vermin covers everything from their New York history to their ecology and from their control to their controllers. Extensive and extended notes add to the more-information-than-you-might-care-to-know nature of this offbeat volume.

Less offbeat than *Rats*, but equally well written, is Sullivan's *The Thoreau You Don't Know*. The book, about he of Walden Pond fame, aims to reveal unfamiliar—or unremembered—aspects of Thoreau's character, laying to rest the clichéd picture of the hermit philosopher and emphasizing, instead, his gregarious nature, natural wit, and love for dancing and singing. Sullivan certainly doesn't stint on other biographical detail, but he manages to bring his own brand of wit to the proceedings. On a highly personal note: Thoreau was also a carpenter who helped build a house for Ralph Waldo Emerson's sister-in-law across the street from the Emerson House. I've had the pleasure of staying in that house a number of times, since it is now owned by friends of mine in Concord, where Thoreau, of course, lived.

ROCKET BOYS

Hickam, Homer H. Delacorte, 1998. ISBN: 038533320X. **B/M, HIST**

Set in the small town of Coalwood, West Virginia, in the 1950s, in the wake of Russia's launch of Sputnik, this affecting memoir captures Hickam's boyhood fascination with rockets and rocket science. Growing up to be a NASA engineer, Hickam is a gifted storyteller who borrows the techniques of fiction (some critics suggested he borrowed a few too many) to write a compelling story that begins in 1957, the year he was 14. Deciding to build a rocket of his own, he enlists the aid of a clutch of friends, and the boys form the Big Creek Missile Agency (BCMA), ultimately building and launching a rocket that soars to an altitude of 31,000 feet. Of course, the road to success is full of potholes, and Hickam describes them all to good comedic and occasionally dramatic effect. A counterpoint to this story of the future is the decline of the West Virginia coal mines, a trend made personal by the fact that Hickam's father was the superintendent of the local mine. While the father dreamed that his son would grow up to be a mining engineer, Homer had different ideas, and his mother, hoping a career in rocket science would help him escape the mines, was an enthusiastic supporter of them. This charming story of overcoming obstacles is enriched by Hickam's portraits of Coalwood locals, many of whom became involved in one way or another with the BCMA. *Rocket Boys* was made into a successful 1998 film titled *October Sky*.

Two years later Hickam published a sequel to *Rocket Boys* titled *The Coalwood Way*. This one finds Hickam a senior in high school who is more interested in dating than in rocketry. However, the decline of the mine continues and tension between the boy's parents grows more tangible. Less successful than *Rocket Boys*, this is nevertheless a lovely and nostalgic evocation of small-town life in the late 1950s.

THE SECRET FAMILY

Bodanis, David. Simon & Schuster, 1997. ISBN: 0684810190. **SCI**

A former academic—he lectured for many years at Oxford University—British author Bodanis has written a fascinating book about a typical day in the life of a typical family of five: mother, father, son, daughter, and infant. His methods, however, are anything but typical. Essentially he puts the family and its environment under a microscope, showing the reader not only the visible world but one that is so tiny as to be invisible to the naked eye. Did you know, for example, that there are upward of ten thousand mites on your pillow? And do you have any idea how many truly disgusting ingredients—chicken feathers and belly stubble from pig carcasses, for example—are added to your food? Yum, yum! He also examines the internal workings of the family's individual bodies and brains, explaining in fascinating detail what motivates and drives us to do the sometimes baffling things we do during a quotidian day. Readers will never look at the world around them in quite the same way again. In his second book, *Electric Universe*, the prolific Bodanis delivers a thoroughly accessible and, indeed, fascinating history of electricity, focusing his attention on the all-too-human scientists and theoreticians, discoverers, and inventors whose work has informed the dynamic field. Expect to find the famous likes of Samuel F. B. Morse (the telegraph) and Alexander Graham Bell (the telephone) in his pages along with the lesser known (Heinrich Hertz, discoverer of radio waves, and William Shockley, he of the transistor).

THE SHALLOWS

Carr, Nicholas. Norton, 2010. ISBN: 9780393072228. **TECH**

An expansion of his influential *Atlantic Monthly* article "Is Google Making Us Stupid?" Carr's book examines in detail the impact of new technology on the human brain and on how we read, process information, and communicate. As the titles of his article and book suggest, the author finds these effects—to put it mildly—not altogether salutary. He argues, for example, that Internet use is having a deleterious impact on our memories and our abilities to concentrate. A chief effect of the latter is our dwindling patience with long-form literature as the Internet trains us—consciously or unconsciously—to desire material presented in outline or bullet form. The result, he claims in his persuasive thematic argument, is a nascent but ongoing rewiring of our brains that will have far-reaching impacts on both individual lives and their social context. Often alarming but essential reading.

SHE'S NOT THERE

Boylan, Jennifer Finney. Broadway Books, 2003. ISBN: 076791404X. **B/M**

Boylan, now cochair of the English Department at Colby College, tells poignantly, candidly, and often humorously of her decision, at age 45, to change her gender. Though born as a male, the conviction that she was "in the wrong body, living the wrong life was never out of my conscious mind—never." How she went about changing from James to Jennifer and its impact on her family—she was married with children—and on her friends—the novelist Richard Russo among them—is an integral part of this fascinating memoir. In her former male self, Boylan was the author of four successful novels (see the entry for James Finney Boylan in the fiction section), and she brings those storytelling skills to her compellingly readable recollections. Reliable and accessible material about transgender and transsexual persons is still limited in our society, as is meaningful discussion of how we define gender, so this book definitely fills a gap. A short story by Boylan—"The Missing Person"— appears in my anthology *How Beautiful the Ordinary*.

SHIP OF GOLD IN THE DEEP BLUE SEA

Kinder, Gary. Atlantic Monthly, 1998. ISBN: 0871134640. **ADV**

Just imagine: a ship, the SS *Central America*, carrying six hundred passengers from the California gold fields in 1857 sinks two hundred miles off the Carolina coast. More than four hundred passengers die in the shipwreck, and twenty-one tons of gold are lost in the worst peacetime shipwreck in American history. This is the raw material that journalist Kinder has to work with, and he definitely makes the most of it in this action-packed story. To the mix he adds the quest, 130 years later, of salvager Tommy Thompson to find the *Central America* and recover the lost gold. In telling his story, Kinder moves backward and forward in time, essentially telling two interrelated stories at once. The fascinating result is another fine example of the current popularity of narrative nonfiction, the kind where you don't want to give away the ending. But just remember that the gold is worth—in contemporary money—a billion dollars, and the ship may be resting on the bottom of the ocean in waters eight thousand feet deep. Can Thompson possibly find it and retrieve the gold?

A SHORT HISTORY OF NEARLY EVERYTHING

Bryson, Bill. Broadway Books, 2003. ISBN: 0767908171. **GNF, SCI, HUM**

The indefatigable and always popular nonfiction author Bryson has, over the years, written about a wild variety of subjects ranging from travel to walking to words. So perhaps it was inevitable that he should, sooner or later, write a book about, well, everything. The genial Bryson begins at the beginning with the big bang and then examines the aftermath, including the ultimate evolu- tion of *Homo sapiens*. Bryson has a wonderful gift for making often abstruse science accessible to the general reader, and YAs will be fascinated by his take on both the cosmic and the comical. To gather his cornucopia of information, Bryson read systematically through the relevant literature and traveled widely to interview the experts in the numerous fields he examined. The result is a delight that *People* magazine called "science with a smile." Readers who'd like more Bryson should look for his classic *A Walk in the Woods*, about his adventures hiking America's Appalachian Trail; or his book *At Home: A Short History of Private Life*, in which he takes a less macroscopic look at the world around him by focusing his close attention on his own home and what it tells him about the evolution of domesticity. All of these are highly recommended.

THE SPOKEN WORD REVOLUTION

Eleveld, Mark, and Marc Smith, eds. Sourcebooks, 2003. ISBN: 1402200374. **P**

As the coeditors of this groundbreaking anthology demonstrate, poetry has come full circle, returning to its oral roots, as it has become a wildly popular performance art. Open mic nights now abound, offering unpublished poets an opportunity to share their work with audiences, and poetry slams have become a popular form of creative competition, one that often provides excellent programming for public libraries. In fact, coeditor Smith, himself a celebrated poet, is the creator of the poetry slam. His coeditor, Eleveld, is a high school teacher in Peoria, Illinois, and a noted champion of oral poetry. In addition to a generous sampling of exemplary work, the editors include essays that trace the history of the form from 1950s Beat poetry to contemporary rap, hip-hop, and other performance art. In 2007 Eleveld edited a second collection, *The Spoken Word Revolution Redux*. This one too is a mixture of poetry and historical and critical essays. In one of these, the former U.S. Poet Laureate Ted Kooser describes performance poetry as "a turning back toward the excitement our ancestors felt as they sat close to the fire and listened to their shaman tell stories."

STITCHES

Small, David. Norton, 2009. ISBN: 9780393068573. **GN, B/M, ALEX**

Presented in graphic novel form, this story of the Caldecott Medal–winning illustrator's young life in the 1950s takes the reader on a harrowing journey into one of the darkest of dark childhoods. With a cold, uncaring mother, an often absent father, and an angry, hostile older brother, Small lived a life of emotional isolation. Worse, when he was a child, he received massive radiation therapy from his radiologist father designed to cure his sinus and breathing difficulties. As a result, he developed cancer and—without being told of his condition—underwent throat surgery at age 14 that left him virtually mute. He left home at 16 to pursue a career as an artist. His evocation of this period in black-and-white drawings and ink washes is absolutely haunting and the situations depicted, often horrifying. It's a wonder that Small survived to create this extraordinary memoir that Françoise Mouly, the art editor of the *New Yorker*, says "breaks new ground for graphic novels." And so it does.

SWIMMING TO ANTARCTICA

Cox, Lynne. Knopf, 2004. ISBN: 0375415076. **B/M, SPO, ALEX**

Cox's first-person account of her extraordinary physical skills and accomplishments as a long-distance swimmer makes for compelling reading. Though she originally planned to become a speed swimmer, Cox quickly discovered a gift for long-distance feats. By the age of 15, in fact, she had already set a new record for crossing the English Channel. She subsequently became the first to swim the Straits of Magellan, caught dysentery from swimming in the garbage-infested Nile, risked shark attack in swimming the Cape of Good Hope, and realized a life's dream when she swam the Bering Strait from Alaska to Russia. Cox is particularly gifted at cold-water swimming—in part, she is the first to acknowledge, because of her degree of insulating body fat. Thus, she was able to negotiate the near-freezing water temperatures of her Anatarctic swim without a wetsuit! Cox's is an amazing story of accomplishment and adventure that has captivated teen readers since its publication.

TRUE NOTEBOOKS

Salzman, Mark. Knopf, 2003. ISBN: 0375413081. **GNF, B/M, ALEX**

As a favor to a friend, Salzman—author of such teen-friendly books as *Iron and Silk* and *Lost in Place*—visited a creative writing class at Los Angeles's Central Juvenile Hall, a lockup for some of LA's most violent juvenile offenders. To his surprise he found the experience so rewarding that he became a volunteer teacher himself. This book is an account of his first two years there. Not only does he offer his examination of the experience along with some beautifully realized verbal portraits of the young men he encountered, so too does he include generous samples of their writing (with their permission), much of it revelatory and much of it excellent in conception and execution. Though he finds the experience wonderfully positive, he acknowledges a pall that hung over each class: the fact that many of his students were accused of such violent crimes—including murder—that they would soon be transferred to adult prisons. This naturally led Salzman to wonder, "What is the value of a positive experience if it is only temporary?" His answer:

> How do you weigh the advantages against the disadvantages of affection, or of aspiration? After all I'd been through with the boys—some of it wonderful and some of it terrible—all I could say was that a little good has to be better than no good at all.

An Alex winner, this book was hailed by *Booklist* as "wonderful." And so it is.

Another YA-friendly title by Salzman is *Lost in Place: Growing Up Absurd in Suburbia*, in which the author recalls his teenage years growing up in Ridgefield, Connecticut. As readers of his earlier book *Iron and Silk* will know, Salzman grew up with a passion for all things Chinese and, as readers of this memoir further learn, was determined to lead the life of a Zen monk as a young adult. He studied Chinese, practiced Chinese brush painting, rigged up a monk outfit, walked barefoot in the snow, and so on, to good eccentric effect. All of this is engagingly and often humorously told, but the real attraction turns out to be Salzman's relationship with his acerbic social worker father, which adds a nice cutting edge to this delightful memoir.

TWEAK: GROWING UP ON METHAMPHETAMINES

Sheff, Nic. Atheneum, 2008. ISBN: 1416913629. **B/M**

Written when he was 22, Sheff's memoir covers much the same ground as his father's (*Beautiful Boy*, above) but with a first-person, present-tense intensity that is unsettling but certainly essential reading for anyone considering using meth, for those who have become addicted, and for their families.

THIS BOY'S LIFE: A MEMOIR

Wolff, Tobias. Atlantic Monthly, 1989. ISBN: 0871132486. **B/M**

Here is *the* classic coming-of-age memoir, though not the first about the Wolff family. That honor goes to Wolff's brother, Geoffrey, and his memoir of their father, the wonderfully titled *The Duke of Deception*. The apple doesn't fall far from the tree, and Tobias Wolff himself proves to be a master of deception, living a life of borderline juvenile delinquency, forging checks, stealing cars, altering school transcripts, and more. Early on, however, he changes his name to Jack to distance himself from his father, even though they live apart. In the meantime he lives a peripatetic life with his mother, who is attracted to abusive men—most notably Dwight Hansen, with whom the family settles in the town of Concrete, Washington, near Seattle. Hansen's most notable contribution to Wolff's adolescence is his attempt to teach the boy to fight (a situation reminiscent of Bil Wright's *Sunday You Learn How to Box*). Jack's life remains unsettled even after he is accepted to an exclusive prep school but, unable to maintain his grades, is expelled in his senior year; he finally joins the army and serves in the Vietnam War. This wonderful memoir was made into a 1993 movie starring Robert De Niro and a very young Leonardo DiCaprio.

THE TIPPING POINT

Gladwell, Malcolm. Little, Brown, 2000. ISBN: 0316316962. **TECH**

New Yorker writer Gladwell's book about trends is one of those rare titles that appear at just the right time to capture the public consciousness and create not only book-selling buzz but also serious discussion and debate. Though not intended as such, *The Tipping Point* became a case study of its own investigation of when and why certain phenomena reach a critical mass, or tipping point, and become what the author describes as "social epidemics." Gladwell found that a surprisingly small number of people (whom he calls mavens, salesmen, and connectors) or even one influential person can create fads and trends both local and national. Among his examples are the sudden decrease in crime in New York, the surprising fad of wearing Hush Puppies, and smoking among young people. The idea that one could control tipping points is ominous as an exercise in public manipulation, and Gladwell's book is an important contribution to sociology and social dynamics. Gladwell is also the author of the best-selling *Blink*, a book about snap decisions made within the first two seconds of observation. Like *The Tipping Point*, this too dissects a phenomenon that could easily lend itself to mass manipulation.

YOU ARE NOT A GADGET

Lanier, Jaron. Knopf, 2010. ISBN: 9780307269645. **TECH**

Lanier, who coined the term *virtual reality*, offers a cautionary look at the pervasiveness of computer technology in our culture and in our commerce. He is particularly concerned about the less than positive impact of Web 2.0, which—he argues—is creating a "hive mind" at the expense of individuality. Among the examples he offers is Wikipedia, with its group efforts at the expense of individual creativity and expository efforts. He is also concerned about the fragmentation of information on the Web that negatively impacts an individual's ability to pursue information and reasoned argument in greater depth. This is an important book for young adults whose lives will be powerfully—and perhaps negatively—affected by the issues Lanier addresses.

WAITING FOR SNOW IN HAVANA: CONFESSIONS OF A CUBAN BOY

Eire, Carlos. Free Press, 2003. ISBN: 0743219651. **B/M, LOI**

Born in Havana in 1950, Eire spent an idyllic childhood as the scion of a wealthy, influential, and occasionally eccentric family. His father, a judge, believed he was the reincarnation of Louis XVI, for example, and the highly religious Eire imagined he saw the face of Jesus at his school window. All of this changed in 1958 when Fidel Castro deposed the Batista regime. Castro, whom Eire calls "Beelzebub, Herod and the Seven-Headed Beast of the Apocalypse rolled into one" outlawed religion, declared Christmas illegal, and sucked the joy out of the 8-year-old Eire's life. Though many of his friends left Cuba in the wake of the revolution, Eire's family remained until 1962, when the author and his brother, along with 14,000 other children, were airlifted to Miami. Eire then lived with foster families for three years until he was reunited with his mother. Sadly, he never saw his father again. Gorgeously written and as compulsively readable as a good novel, Eire's critically praised memoir won the 2003 National Book Award in the nonfiction category. Published in 2010, a sequel, *Learning to Die in Miami: Confessions of a Refugee Boy*, recounts Eire's early years in America, focusing on his attempts to acculturate and become a "real" American. The author is now a professor of history and religious studies at Yale, where he received his PhD.

WHEN I WAS PUERTO RICAN / ALMOST A WOMAN

Santiago, Esmeralda. Addison Wesley, 1993.

ISBN: 0201581175 / Perseus, 1998. ISBN: 0738200433. **B/M, LOI, ALEX**

Consider these two volumes a single memoir rather than separate books. Together they eloquently tell the story of Santiago's early childhood in Puerto Rico, her arrival at age 13 in the Brooklyn barrio, and her life there during the 1960s. The eldest of eleven children, she and her family often live in poverty, and as is often the case, the girl has to assume adult responsibilities at a young age, acting as a translator for her single-parent mother and struggling to find a home between two worlds. Her life starts to change when she is accepted to New York's prestigious Performing Arts High School and begins to pursue acting opportunities while at the same time trying to develop a persona apart from her strong-willed Mami. The author writes candidly about her sexual coming-of-age and her relationships with a number of different men, most important, a Turkish filmmaker. It is her affair with him that ultimately is the catalyst for her decision to find an independent life. Santiago's is a classic story of acculturation and growing up in America. Readers might want to compare Santiago's two-volume memoir with that of Marjane Satrapi's Persepolis memoirs (above), as well as Nicholasa Mohr's short story collections, *El Bronx Remembered* and *In Nueva York*.

APPENDIX A

NOT TO BE MISSED

BOOKS NOTABLE FOR
THEIR OVERALL EXCELLENCE

FICTION

All the Pretty Horses by Cormac McCarthy

The Amazing Adventures of Kavalier and Clay by Michael Chabon

Black Hole by Charles Burns

Black Swan Green by David Mitchell

The Brief Wondrous Life of Oscar Wao by Junot Díaz

The Client by John Grisham

A Complicated Kindness by Miriam Toews

The Curious Incident of the Dog in the Night-Time by Mark Haddon

Extremely Loud and Incredibly Close by Jonathan Safran Foer

The Girl Who Loved Tom Gordon by Stephen King

The Kite Runner by Khaled Hosseini

A Lesson before Dying by Ernest J. Gaines

Life of Pi by Yann Martel

The Lovely Bones by Alice Sebold

Mister Pip by Lloyd Jones

Montana 1948 by Larry Watson

More Like Not Running Away by Paul Shepherd

The Outside Boy by Jeanine Cummins

The Perks of Being a Wallflower by Stephen Chbosky

Plainsong by Kent Haruf

Rule of the Bone by Russell Banks

The Secret Life of Bees by Sue Monk Kidd

Stardust by Neil Gaiman

The Story of Edgar Sawtelle by David Wroblewski

The Things They Carried by Tim O'Brien

To Say Nothing of the Dog by Connie Willis
When We Get There by Shauna Seliy
Wicked by Gregory Maguire

NONFICTION

Age of Bronze by Eric Shanower
And the Pursuit of Happiness by Maria Kalman
Angela's Ashes by Frank McCourt
Blankets by Craig Thompson
The Calvin and Hobbes *Tenth Anniversary Book* by Bill Watterson
Columbine by Dave Cullen
The Devil in the White City by Erik Larson
Epileptic by David B.
Fun Home by Alison Bechdel
Into Thin Air by Jon Krakauer
Kampung Boy by Lat
Me Talk Pretty One Day by David Sedaris
Nickle and Dimed by Barbara Ehrenreich
One Hundred Demons by Lynda Barry
The Perfect Storm by Sebastian Junger
Persepolis by Marjane Satrapi
Stitches by David Small
This Boy's Life by Tobias Wolff

APPENDIX B

SOMETHING ENTIRELY DIFFERENT

BOOKS NOTABLE FOR THEIR ORIGINALITY

FICTION

As Simple as Snow by Gregory Galloway

Citrus County by John Brandon

The Curious Incident of the Dog in the Night-Time by Mark Haddon

Elmer by Gerry Alanguilan

Extremely Loud and Incredibly Close by Jonathan Safran Foer

Jamrach's Menagerie by Carol Birch

JPod by Douglas Coupland

Life of Pi by Yann Martel

The Perks of Being a Wallflower by Stephen Chbosky

Pygmy by Chuck Palahniuk

Shades of Grey by Jasper Fforde

Special Topics in Calamity Physics by Marisha Pessl

The Story of Edgar Sawtelle by David Wroblewski

Swamplandia! by Karen Russell

Wicked by Gregory Maguire

Wonder When You'll Miss Me by Amanda Davis

NONFICTION

Age of Bronze by Eric Shanower

American Voyeur by Benoit Denizet-Lewis

And the Pursuit of Happiness by Maira Kalman

Ardency by Kevin Young

Fun Home by Alison Bechdel

I Am an Emotional Creature by Eve Ensler

Jesus Land by Julia Scheeres

Kampung Boy by Lat

Logicomix by Apostolos Doxiadis and Christos H. Papadimitriou

Packing for Mars by Mary Roach
Persepolis by Marjane Satrapi
Rats by Robert Sullivan
The Secret Family by David Bodanis
She's Not There by Jennifer Finney Boylan
Stitches by David Small

INDEX

You may also be interested in

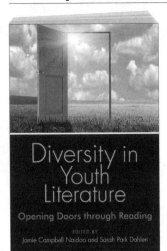

DIVERSITY IN YOUTH LITERATURE
Opening Doors through Reading

Edited by Jamie Campbell Naidoo and Sarah Park Dahlen

This thoughtful and timely book helps meet the informational, recreational, and cultural needs of today's youth and those who serve them.

ISBN: 978-0-8389-1143-3
224 pp / 6" × 9"

**YOUNG ADULT
LITERATURE**
MICHAEL CART
ISBN: 978-0-8389-1045-0

**TECHNOLOGY
AND LITERACY**
JENNIFER NELSON AND
KEITH BRAAFLADT
ISBN: 978-0-8389-1108-2

TEEN CRAFT PROJECTS 2
TINA COLEMAN AND
PEGGIE LLANES
ISBN: 978-0-8389-1152-5

**BOOKLIST'S 1000 BEST
YOUNG ADULT BOOKS,
2000–2010**
EDITORS OF BOOKLIST
ISBN: 978-0-8389-1150-1

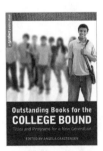

**OUTSTANDING BOOKS
FOR THE COLLEGE BOUND**
EDITED BY ANGELA CARSTENSEN
FOR YALSA
ISBN: 978-0-8389-8570-0

**MULTICULTURAL
PROGRAMS FOR
TWEENS AND TEENS**
EDITED BY LINDA B. ALEXANDER
AND NAHYUN KWON
FOR YALSA
ISBN: 978-0-8389-3582-8